Leaders Guide

Creating Quality RELATIONSHIPS
IN A FAST-PACED WORLD

By
Denny Rydberg

Group
Books

Loveland, Colorado

Acknowledgments

I want to thank the 1986-87 and 1987-88 University Ministries Staff for their contribution: Steve and Lisa Call, Rod Handley, Stu Harris, Lisa Kragerud, David Parker, Marti Shefveland, Carolyn Duffy, Mike Gaffney, Mark Hogendobler, Kara Holmes, Eric Lingren, Sean Shannon, Bruce and Gay Bailey, Marilyn Rydberg, Laura Swain and Jo Anne Wood.

Special thanks to teammate Rod Handley for his significant involvement.

Dedication

To my daughter Heather.

Creating Quality Relationships in a Fast-Paced World: Leaders Guide

Copyright © 1988 by Denny Rydberg

First Printing

All rights reserved. No part of this book may be reproduced in any manner whatsoever without written permission from the publisher except where noted in the text and in the case of brief quotations embodied in critical articles and reviews. For information write Permissions, Group Books, Box 481, Loveland, CO 80539.

Credits

Edited by Nancy M. Shaw

Designed by Judy Atwood

Scripture quotations are from the Holy Bible, New International Version. Copyright © 1973, 1978, 1984 International Bible Society. Used by permission of Zondervan Bible Publishers.

"Flexibility Checklist" in Study 6 reprinted with permission from *Whatever Happened to Marriage*, by Denny Rydberg, a LifeStyle elective for young adults. © 1976 David C. Cook Publishing Co., Elgin, IL 60120.

"How to Relate to Your Parents" worksheet in Study 8 taken from *Beyond Graduation* by Denny Rydberg. To be published by Zondervan Publishing House, Spring 1988. All rights reserved. Used by permission.

Material in Study 9 adapted from *The Birth Order Book* by Kevin Leman, copyright © 1985 by Dr. Kevin Leman. Used by permission of Fleming H. Revell Company.

"A Picture of Jesus" and "Stages of a Spiritual Journal" in Study 11 were adapted from *The Serendipity Bible Study Book* by Lyman Coleman, Denny Rydberg, Richard Peace & Gary Christopherson, © 1986 by Zondervan Publishing House. Used by permission.

"Five Stages of a Spiritual Journey" in Study 12 is adapted from *All the Way* (Serendipity Youth Bible Study Series) by Lyman Coleman and Denny Rydberg, © 1982 by Serendipity House. Used by permission.

ISBN 0931-529-34-4

Printed in the United States of America

Contents

Introduction

*Y*oung adults are concerned about relationships. They ask questions such as "How do I become my own best friend? How can I develop friendships that last? How can I establish a relationship of love and romance with a member of the opposite sex? What makes a good marriage? How can I find fulfillment as a single person? How do I get along on my job? How can I improve relationships with my brothers and sisters? How do I relate to my parents now that I'm an adult? How do I establish and keep my spiritual relationship fresh?"

Young adults want their current relationships to be healthier. They want to know what it means to be a good friend, a good employer or employee and a good husband or wife. They also want a relationship with Christ that is not "lukewarm."

THE STUDIES

Creating Quality Relationships in a Fast-Paced World is a 12-session curriculum that helps young adults evaluate and discuss their relationships. Each session covers a specific topic such as the need for relationships, accepting yourself, friendship, dating, marriage, singleness, relationships with family members and individuals within the work place, and the unique relationship with Christ.

Each study session is:

- **student-centered.** In other words, students are actively involved. Their thoughts, participation and interaction with one another make this course effective. The leader is merely a guide rather than a special lecturer or an "all-knowing" teacher. This distinction encourages discussion because it makes everyone a learner.

- **discussion-centered.** Young adults want to talk. They are much more willing to express their thoughts and opinions than high school or junior high young people and aren't nearly as inhibited as older adults. They're ready to share.

Even though other "creative strategies" are employed, most of these studies are centered around discussion. Thought-provoking questions initiate quality discussions. As the Holy Spirit expresses himself through individual contributions, participants feel encouraged to share their thoughts and insights as part of the body of Christ.

- **Christ-centered.** In Ephesians 1:10, Paul writes that God's plan is "to bring all things in heaven and on earth together under one head, even Christ." Christ helps clarify things; therefore, biblical content is emphasized because it clarifies how relationships should operate.

THE FORMAT

The studies in *Creating Quality Relationships in a Fast-Paced World* are flexible in format. You can use these 55-minute studies as a 12-week Sunday morning curriculum, or you can emphasize one section at a time as the study portion for a retreat. Use all materials for a midweek series of meetings, or choose individual studies for intensive small groups. The choice is up to you.

This curriculum offers easy-to-use materials that require little preparation. The Leaders Guide offers background information, programming materials and practical tips on how to use the studies most effectively. Plus participants have their own Study Guides that contain worksheets and homework activities.

These studies can be lengthened easily by allowing more time for discussion on each question. Sessions also can be shortened by deleting worksheets or asking participants to work on the materials at home. Feel free to adapt the time segments to your own needs, being responsive to those special moments of sharing that will occur within your group.

Each study is introduced by a list of objectives and tips for preparation. The programming part of each study is based on three distinct parts:

Opening—a short activity or discussion question that stimulates participants to talk about a particular relationship.

Exploration—various forms of study, including worksheets, activities and Bible study, that promote small group interaction and discussion.

Closing—some form of personal affirmation or dedication that encourages a response to each study such as celebrating one's personal gifts or sharing a decision on how to respond to a family member.

To enhance each study, there is further opportunity for personal growth in the "Solo" activities. These homework pages in the Study Guide spark suggestions for personal evaluation and provide activities that encourage thinking and a response. Additional readings also are suggested in each study for those who want to pursue the subject further.

This material will help you and your young adults find answers to many of their questions and encourage everyone to live relationally as well. God bless you and your young adults as you struggle together with how to develop healthier relationships.

The Death of the Lone Ranger

*W*hy do people need friendships? Why can't individuals exist by themselves? If friendships are necessary, why are they so difficult and distorted at times and so good at other times?

This study will deal with these questions and more. Relationships are one of God's great ideas. When he created human beings, he planned for individuals to relate well to him, to others, to his creation and to themselves. The bad news about this plan is that sin has caused relationships to suffer. But the good news is that God continues to make relationships work. This first study looks at both the good and bad news about relationships and sets the framework for the following studies.

OBJECTIVES

In this study participants will:

● realize individuals can't exist by themselves—people need each other.

● investigate the basics for meaningful relationships.

● begin the process of committing themselves to a group of people who will care for each other and learn together over the next 12 sessions.

PREPARATION ....

☐ Study the material carefully and prayerfully.

☐ Gather one Study Guide and pencil for each participant. You'll also need newsprint and a marker.

☐ Choose someone to read aloud "The Lone Ranger and Me." Not everyone is a good reader in public nor does everyone feel comfortable reading aloud, so choose a person in advance.

OPENING

(10 minutes) Welcome everyone, then explain that this is a 12-week course about relationships. Distribute the Study Guides and pencils. Ask participants to turn to the contents and follow along as you briefly highlight the studies. Then say: "Throughout this course, we don't want to just *talk* about relationships, we also want to *develop* relationships. To begin that process, let's introduce ourselves by saying our name and answering these questions: 'When you were growing up, what was one of your favorite TV programs, and what do you remember about the atmosphere in which you watched it?' For example, were you with family or friends? Did you watch it in a particular room? Did you snack while watching the program?"

Even with groups of more than 15 people, this activity can be done quickly if people briefly answer the questions. Set the stage for quick answers by simply stating your name and briefly answering the questions. This gives other members of the group a chance to think of an answer and feel more comfortable. This activity helps break the ice, brings back a few memories and creates some bonds with a new group of people.

EXPLORATION

(10 minutes) Thank everyone for sharing. Then say, "Let's begin this course by first talking about friendships." Lead a large group discussion using the following questions:

1. What are the benefits of a good friendship? (Some benefits you

can mention are encouragement; support; companionship; personal effectiveness; sharing; vulnerability; protection; insight into others, God and self.)

2. Is it more difficult for you to be friends with members of the same sex or the opposite sex? Explain.

3. Do you think the quality of friendships is better today in our culture than it has been in the past? Why or why not?

4. What are some obstacles to friendships today?

(13 minutes) Wrap up the discussion by telling the group: "Each week as we study relationships, we'll use a different approach. Sometimes we'll participate in small groups. Sometimes we'll study the Bible more than usual. Sometimes we'll listen to short lectures. Today, we're going to read and respond to a story. Let's turn to 'The Lone Ranger and Me.' " Signal the person you'd asked earlier to read aloud "The Lone Ranger and Me." Encourage group members to take notes as they hear the story (items they question, agree with, disagree with, want more information about, don't understand, etc.).

The Lone Ranger and Me ▬▬▬▬▬▬▬▬

Instructions: Take notes in the space provided as a person reads this story.

Notes:

When I was a kid, my favorite TV program was *The Lone Ranger*, a weekly series. My cousin Pat and I would watch it at Grandpa and Grandma's on their black and white TV set since neither my parents nor Pat's owned one. Pat and I would involve ourselves in any program, but *The Lone Ranger* was special. Each week, I would be the Lone Ranger as we watched and Pat would be Tonto, the Lone Ranger's trusty sidekick. (I was the oldest, so I got to choose the character I wanted.) For 30 minutes, we would absorb the program and then go out and relive it in Grandma's neighborhood.

It was always the same formula. Some folks (ranchers, farmers, townspeople or settlers) would be picked on by the bad guys. But then the Lone Ranger appeared and rescued the people in less than 30 minutes (so there would still be time for a Cheerios commercial). In the process, the Lone Ranger never took off his mask (although the bad guys were often trying to do that). He'd leave his trademark, a silver bullet, as a reminder as he left town with a command to his horse, "Heigh-ho, Silver, away!" Tonto's horse's name was Scout, but Tonto never yelled, "Heigh-ho, Scout!" He did call the Lone Ranger "Kemo Sabe." I never did get an accurate translation on that.

The Lone Ranger never developed significant relationships with any of the people he helped. He was simply a savior who rescued people and then rode off into the sunset. Even in his relationship with Tonto, the Lone Ranger revealed very little about himself. He never seemed to need much help. The Lone Ranger was so resourceful he could single-handedly save almost anyone and could solve almost any problem.

I remember a joke about the Lone Ranger when he was in desperate straits. A band of 100 Apaches had surrounded him and Tonto. The Lone Ranger turned to his trusted Indian companion and announced, "Tonto, we're in deep trouble!"

Tonto replied, "What do you mean *we*, paleface?"

Maybe the Lone Ranger didn't even have a close relationship with Tonto. How would we ever know?

Thank the reader, then lead a discussion by asking the group these questions:

1. How many of you remember *The Lone Ranger* or a series similar to it? Describe some of your memories.

2. What were some of the questions or notes you wrote during the reading?

3. Which of the following characters are you most like, and why?
a. The Lone Ranger
b. Tonto
c. Townspeople
d. Bad guys

4. How is life today like the life portrayed in *The Lone Ranger* series? Can one person depend only on himself or herself? Why or why not? Does life always have happy endings? Explain.

Say: "Somehow, in our high-tech culture, the cult of the Lone Ranger has survived. We want to be independent, needing no one. We want to be Lone Rangers without even a Tonto. We want to be personally resourceful. But after we've tried that for a while, we realize that the Lone Ranger is dead. His 'solo act' is not the way to live. Some of us, however, have lived like the Lone Ranger for so long that we know very little about quality relationships. Some of us have a few good relationships, but we'd like to make them better. That's what this course is all about—how to make relationships work. Relationships with yourself, peers, parents, employers, fellow workers and God. So to begin, let's take a look at a biblical understanding of relationships."

(13 minutes) Divide into small groups of three to four people. Have everyone turn to "Thoughts About Relationships." Ask the small groups to follow the directions and discuss the questions.

Thoughts About Relationships ▬▬▬▬▬▬▬

Instructions: In your small group, read each thought and answer the questions.

Thought 1: In the beginning, God created men and women for the purpose of friendship and fellowship. God desired to share himself and his creation—with men and women. That initial friendship between God and humanity was ideal and uninterrupted and is described in the early chapters of Genesis. There was only one peril that could contaminate that relationship: sin. Sin entered the world and the harmony between God and humans, between humans and humans, and between humans and nature disintegrated. Disharmony reigned. (Read Genesis 1—3 for this story.)

a. How would you describe the disharmony that resulted from Adam and Eve's disobedience? _____

_____

b. How do people place barriers in their relationship with God today? _____

_____

Thought 2: Since that time, relationships have been distorted. Men and women long for the harmony and for the intimate relationships with God and with each other that existed in the Garden of Eden. The sin that destroyed the purity of these relationships and caused so much confusion and disharmony is referred to by theologians as the Fall of Man. The Fall not only separated people from God but also people from each other. This disharmony and disunity escalated so quickly that in the next generation, Adam and Eve's son Cain murdered his brother Abel. (Read Genesis 4 for that sad story.)

Even though people longed for relationships, sin had begun to warp the way people attempted to love and care for one another. Selfishness increased. Cain, for instance, felt he no longer needed Abel. And in anger, Cain killed Abel. An ugly, selfish attitude began in just the second generation of humanity.

a. What did Cain mean when he asked, "Am I my brother's keeper?" Have you ever felt this way? Explain. _____

_____

b. How does a "looking out for #1" attitude affect our relationships? _____

_____

Thought 3: Today, that attitude has been perpetuated. We still spend much of our time looking out for #1 and, consequently, our relationships suffer. When we pretend to be self-sufficient and independent like the Lone Ranger, we build tall, thick walls around ourselves and post signs that say:

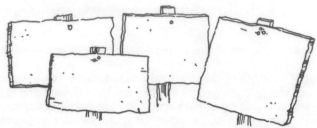

a. What other signs would you add? (Take a moment to fill in the blank signs.)

b. Share one of your statements in your small group.

As a large group, discuss answers and feelings that resulted from the worksheet. Ask those who feel comfortable to share some of their "signs" that prevent quality relationships.

(5 minutes) Tell the group: "We erect these signs both verbally and non-verbally. Often, people who most emphatically make these statements are desperately seeking a friend or some other outlet to fill the void of emptiness. When relationships sour, the void may be filled with an appetite for counterfeit outlets such as alcohol, drugs, money, power and fame.

"What humans have done with relationships is much different from what God intended. Consequently, we have trouble in relationships. We need to get back to the basics. We need to discover how God wants us to relate to others. Turn to 'Back to the Basics With Relationships.' After I read each passage, call out the basic guidelines it gives us about relationships. I'll write your ideas on newsprint. In the space provided on your worksheet, note any basic guidelines you'd like to remember." Mention some basics such as learn to love yourself so you can love others, give of yourself, or take your focus off yourself and place it on others.

Back to the Basics With Relationships ▬▬▬▬▬

Instructions: What does the Bible say about relationships? Note any guidelines and thoughts that will help you get back to the basics in your relationships.

1. "A friend loves at all times, and a brother is born for adversity" (Proverbs 17:17).

Basic guidelines:

2. "Two are better than one, because they have a good return for their work: If one falls down, his friend can help him up. But pity the man who falls and has no one to help him up! Also, if two lie down together, they will keep warm. But how can one keep warm alone? Though one may be overpowered, two can defend themselves. A cord of three strands is not quickly broken" (Ecclesiastes 4:9-12).

Basic guidelines:

3. "A new command I give you: Love one another. As I have loved you, so you must love one another. By this all men will know that you are my disciples, if you love one another" (John 13:34-35).

Basic guidelines:

4. "Greater love has no one than this, that he lay down his life for his friends" (John 15:13).

Basic guidelines:

Say: "Think about these basic guidelines for better relationships. Which one of these basics would you like to apply to your life? Choose a person sitting closest to you and tell him or her about it."

CLOSING

(4 minutes) After partners finish discussing, gather in a circle and stack hands in the center for a closing prayer. Ask everyone to bow their heads and picture one person with whom they'd like to build a better relationship. Pray: "Heavenly Father, help us take off the masks that prevent people from knowing us. Help us realize we need each other. Thanks for your Word and your guidelines for relationships. Help us love one another as you have loved us. Amen."

Ask participants to take their Study Guides home and complete the "Solo" assignment for Study 1 sometime during the next week. Encourage them to focus on the relationships they want to improve during the next three months. Tell participants to bring back their Study Guides for each session.

Remind everyone the next topic will be "Created to Relate." Encourage individuals to read Josh McDowell's book *His Image . . . My Image* (Here's Life) as they begin to think about what this means.

Solo

Instructions: Complete the following chart. Decide on two relationships you'd like to improve and list specific ways you can improve them. Be honest and specific. For example, you may want to improve your relationship with your dad. Specific ways to work on this relationship could be to call him every week, write him a letter once a month or set up a time to visit him. At the end of this course, see how your relationships have improved.

Relationship A	Ways to Improve It
	1. 2. 3. 4.
Relationship B	**Ways to Improve It**
	1. 2. 3. 4.

Created to Relate

*H*ow can individuals learn to recognize their value? How should God's view affect the way people feel about themselves and how they relate to others?

After God created the universe and all its creatures, he felt a need for something more—a special kind of relationship. So he created human beings—"male and female he created them." Recognizing the potential of these creations, God shared his plan with them and offered them an opportunity to choose to be part of that plan.

God continues to offer that choice to individuals every day. When people accept a relationship with God, they find value and meaning in what they do and say. Recognizing their personal value in God's eyes gives individuals the strength to be what they were created to be—children of God. Encourage young adults to enter this study looking for new ways to evaluate their self-worth.

OBJECTIVES

In this study participants will:

- reflect and focus on who they were created to be.
- look at how much God loves and values them.
- focus on the concept of affirmation.
- continue to build a learning, caring and supportive community.

PREPARATION ·

☐ Study the material carefully and prayerfully.
☐ Gather pencils, 3×5 cards, Bibles and extra Study Guides.

OPENING

(5 minutes) Welcome the group. Explain that this is only the second week of the relationship series so newcomers should feel they can easily catch up and take part in the study. Briefly review last week's study and describe the course as a whole. (See the introductions for the course and for Study 1.) Pass out pencils and distribute Study Guides to those who don't have them.

EXPLORATION

(5 minutes) Say: "When Jesus was asked what was the most important commandment or teaching of all, he said: 'Love the Lord your God with all your heart and with all your soul and with all your mind and with all your strength. The second is this: Love your neighbor as yourself. There is no commandment greater than these' (Mark 12:30-31).

"Basically he said: 'First, you love God; then you love yourself. For you can only love your neighbor if you know how to love yourself.'

"Think about one of your most successful moments as a child. Maybe you were named captain of the school's safety patrol or you won the spelling bee in your class. Perhaps you starred in the church Christmas pageant or organized the youth group's Thanksgiving food drive. Maybe you listened to a friend and helped her put her life back together. Divide into twos and share what you did that made you feel successful and valuable." Make sure everyone has someone to talk to.

After a few minutes, get the group's attention and say: "Now ask yourself, 'What specific action or personal quality made me feel good about myself? Was I brave? honest? tenderhearted?' Think about that one quality you displayed that would make you valuable as a friend."

(10 minutes) Ask participants to turn to "The Basis for Personal Value." Ask four volunteers to read the thoughts, and encourage the other participants to take notes as they listen.

The Basis for Personal Value ▬▬▬▬▬▬▬▬▬▬

Instructions: Listen carefully as others read the following thoughts. Take notes and record your responses as they read. Be prepared to share your reactions with the rest of the group.

Thought 1: In a society that holds up the illusion of flawless beauty, high intelligence and exceptional career success as the attainable goal, it is no wonder that the reflection we see in the mirror gives negative messages to us such as "Not acceptable," "Unsuccessful," "Don't call us; we'll call you" or "Forget it, chump." We can falsely conclude that if we don't measure up to the world's standards of success, we are not worthy or even lovable. Our negative feelings begin to snowball, and soon our self-worth plummets.
✏️ Notes:

Thought 2: This process begins early in childhood. Out of a desire to have others love and accept us, we learn early how to get attention or praise by using our talents and skills, by looking cute or by performing well. Although the processes of learning acceptable behavior, developing skills and talents and understanding good grooming are very important, these characteristics alone aren't enough to establish a secure sense of self-worth.
✏️ Notes:

Thought 3: No matter how strong or gifted you are, evaluating your personal worth based on external appearance, performance, intelligence or talent will fail you. For comparison is at the heart of this value system. You can always meet someone smarter, prettier, funnier or stronger than you. To maintain your valuable image, you will find that you must excel beyond reason or isolate yourself to a limited environment where you can maintain your position. Evaluating personal worth on this kind of "conditional acceptance" doesn't produce the kind of person you would want to live with in a friendship! This type of atmosphere does not allow for growth or love.
✏️ Notes:

Thought 4: Self-worth needs to be established on solid ground. The heart of the Christian message is God's declaration of our worth. We did not have to perform, achieve or charm our way into God's love for us. Romans 5:8 states God's position: "But God demonstrates his own love for us in this: While we were still sinners, Christ died for us."
✏️ Notes:

Ask: "How did you react to what you just heard? With what do you agree or disagree?" After some brief responses, say: "Let's take a look at what God says about our self-worth. To do that, we're going to break into small groups and work together."

(20 minutes) Encourage participants to divide randomly into three groups. Ask all groups to turn to "Strong Words From God About Who I Am." Assign one section of the worksheet to each small group. Ask them to read the Bible verses and rewrite the ideas into positive statements, or affirmations, about themselves. Remind groups that the point of this activity is to try to understand God's thoughts about us as individuals.

Strong Words From God About Who I Am ▰▰▰▰

Instructions: Read and discuss the section assigned to your small group. Reword the scripture passages into affirmations, or positive statements, about yourself. List situations where each affirmation might prove helpful. Look over the following example:

"For God did not give us a spirit of timidity, but a spirit of power, of love and of self-discipline" (2 Timothy 1:7).

Affirmation: God didn't create me to be shy and withdrawn. He gave me strength, the ability to love others and the skills to discipline myself to use my gifts.

In what situations might this affirmation prove helpful? When I am unsure about myself, when I feel I have little to offer, when I compare myself with others.

When your group is finished, respond individually to the Key Questions on Self-Worth at the end of this worksheet.

1. I am God's creation . . .
a. as a human being.
"So God created man in his own image, in the image of God he created him; male and female he created them" (Genesis 1:27).

Affirmation: _____
_____
_____

b. as an individual.
"For you created my inmost being; you knit me together in my mother's womb" (Psalm 139:13).

Affirmation: _____
_____
_____

c. as a unique Christian.
"But because of his great love for us, God, who is rich in mercy, made us alive with Christ even when we were dead in transgressions—it is by grace you have been saved" (Ephesians 2:4-5).

Affirmation: _____
_____
_____

In what situations might these affirmations prove helpful? _____

_____

What can you conclude from these verses? _____

_____

2. I am the object of God's love and forgiveness, . . .

a. which is demonstrated through the sacrifice of Christ. The worth of something can be determined by who values it and by what someone is willing to sacrifice for it.

"But God demonstrates his own love for us in this: While we were still sinners, Christ died for us" (Romans 5:8).

Affirmation: _____

_____

b. which is demonstrated through establishing an eternal belonging to God.

"For he chose us in him before the creation of the world to be holy and blameless in his sight. In love he predestined us to be adopted as his sons through Jesus Christ . . . And he made known to us the mystery of his will . . . to be put into effect when the times will have reached their fulfillment—to bring all things in heaven and on earth together under one head, even Christ" (Ephesians 1:4-5a, 9a, 10).

Affirmation: _____

_____

In what situations might these affirmations prove helpful? _____

_____

What can you conclude from these verses?_____

_____

3. I am an agent of God's purpose . . .
a. as a temple of God.

"Therefore, I urge you, brothers, in view of God's mercy, to offer your bodies as living sacrifices, holy and pleasing to God—this is your spiritual act of worship" (Romans 12:1).

Affirmation: _____

_____

_____

"For we are the temple of the living God" (2 Corinthians 6:16b).

Affirmation: _____

_____

_____

b. as one who is created for good works.

"No temptation has seized you except what is common to man. And God is faithful; he will not let you be tempted beyond what you can bear. But when you are tempted, he will also provide a way out so that you can stand up under it" (1 Corinthians 10:13).

Affirmation: _____

_____

_____

"And God is able to make all grace abound to you, so that in all things at all times, having all that you need, you will abound in every good work" (2 Corinthians 9:8).

Affirmation: _____

_____

_____

"For we are God's workmanship, created in Christ Jesus to do good works, which God prepared in advance for us to do" (Ephesians 2:10).

Affirmation: _____

_____

_____

c. as one who is gifted uniquely.

"But to each one of us grace has been given as Christ apportioned it. This is why it says: 'When he ascended on high, he led captives in his train and gave gifts to men' . . . It was he who gave some to be apostles, some to be prophets, some to be evangelists, and some to be pastors and teachers, to prepare God's people for works of service, so that the body of Christ may be built up . . ." (Ephesians 4:7-8, 11-12).

Affirmation: _____
_____
_____

d. as one with an eternal destiny.

"I pray also that the eyes of your heart may be enlightened in order that you may know the hope to which he has called you, the riches of his glorious inheritance in the saints, and his incomparably great power for us who believe. That power is like the working of his mighty strength, which he exerted in Christ when he raised him from the dead and seated him at his right hand in the heavenly realms, far above all rule and authority, power and dominion, and every title that can be given, not only in the present age but also in the one to come" (Ephesians 1:18-21).

Affirmation: _____
_____
_____

In what situations might these affirmations prove helpful? _____
_____

What can you conclude from these verses? _____
_____

Key Questions on Self-Worth:

1. What other scripture passages can you use to affirm your life?

2. How important is it to base your self-concept on what God says about you? Explain. How can this decision affect you on a daily basis?

Have participants remain in their small groups and share some of their findings and conclusions with the other groups. Discuss the conclusions in each of the three sections. Ask for volunteers to share their answers to the Key Questions.

(10 minutes) Ask participants to turn to "Steps Toward a Healthy Sense of Self-Worth."

Steps Toward a Healthy Sense of Self-Worth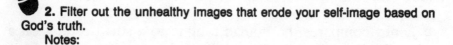

Instructions: Think about these steps and their explanations. Take notes on what you think and feel about each step. Think of examples of how you or others have accomplished these steps.

1. Accept yourself on the basis of God's love and forgiveness toward you.
Notes:

2. Filter out the unhealthy images that erode your self-image based on God's truth.
Notes:

3. Affirm the truth about yourself.
Notes:

Encourage everyone to listen carefully and take notes. Read each step and the explanation that follows. You may want to use examples from your own experience to amplify different points.

Read the first step: "Accept yourself on the basis of God's love and forgiveness toward you." Then say: "God created you. You are loved, forgiven and accepted in Christ. You are offered the gifts of the Holy Spirit. God wants you to know and experience his love. He wants you to believe his messages instead of the negative messages that bombard you. The truest statement about you is what God says." Allow time for participants to record their thoughts.

Read the second step: "Filter out the unhealthy images that erode your self-image based on God's truth." Then say: "When you receive negative messages like 'You're worthless,' 'You're no good,' 'You'll never amount to anything' or 'This is the worst mistake of all,' remind yourself of the truth of God's love and acceptance. If you need to eliminate or forgive some sin, do it quickly. Christ died so you wouldn't have to struggle under a pile of sin and guilt. Reflect on last week's study and remind yourself of what God thinks of you." Again allow time for participants to record their thoughts and feelings.

Read the third step: "Affirm the truth about yourself." Then remind the group: "An affirmation is a positive statement you make about yourself. We are bombarded by so many negative messages that it is good to hear and say the truth. Remember, what you say can affect what you believe about yourself.

"Listen to the following scripture passages. What do you hear about the power of what people say?" Ask three people to read Proverbs 10:11; 18:21; and James 3:2-10. Then ask, "What can you conclude about the power of speech from these verses?"

Listen for these responses:

● James compares the human tongue to a small rudder on a large ship. The mouth is the steering mechanism in a person's life.

● What people say programs their subconscious and influences their feelings, attitudes and perceptions. From a spiritual point of view, what individuals say influences their ability to receive God's power and direction in their lives.

● When people speak the truth in a positive manner, they are agreeing with God and exhibiting faith. When individuals speak negatively or believe untruths about themselves, they are, in essence, disagreeing with God and denying his truth.

CLOSING

(5 minutes) After people share what they heard from the scripture passages, tell the group: "Affirmations are not gimmicks. These positive statements are based on the biblical principle that the tongue is the steering mechanism for the whole personality. Affirmations recognize that death and life are in the power of the tongue. Consequently, we become not only what we think, but also what we say."

Pass a 3×5 card to each person within the small groups. Say: "Write one or more of God's affirmations on your 3×5 card. Carry the card with you during the following week to remind yourself of who you are in God's eyes."

Close with the following prayer: "God, thank you for creating us as valuable individuals. Keep us aware of your love and forgiveness. Use us as valuable agents of your purposes. Remind us to continue to see our value in you. In the name of him whose sacrifice made each one of us valuable, Jesus Christ, amen."

Ask participants to take their Study Guides home, complete the "Solo" assignment and bring their Study Guides back for the next session. Ask individuals to think of ways to remember God's affirmations. Let them know the next study will concentrate on how they can become their own best friend. Encourage them to continue reading *His Image . . . My Image.*

Solo

Instructions: Celebrate who you are! Pick one quality you like about yourself and celebrate it as a gift from God. Write a thank-you note to God and let him know how this quality has impacted your life.

How to Be My Own Best Friend

*A*s a creation of God, how can I learn to be my own best friend? Self-worth and personal acceptance are two of the most critical issues young adults face. Individuals want to know how they can develop a healthy self-respect that won't change with the whims of friends or the trends of the world. Encourage young adults to enter this study looking for ways to strengthen their self-image and better love themselves.

OBJECTIVES
In this study participants will:
- discover what it means to be their own best friend.
- discuss practical tips for being their own best friend.
- continue to build a learning and caring community.

PREPARATION ·

☐ Study the material carefully and prayerfully.
☐ Gather pencils and Bibles.

OPENING

(10 minutes) Welcome the group. Introduce this study by saying: "This week we're going to look at what it means to be your own best friend. Take a moment to think about yourself. If you were to die suddenly, how would you want others to remember you?

"Turn to 'My Epitaph.' Think about how you would summarize your life. Write an epitaph for your gravestone. Remember, epitaphs must be brief. You don't have unlimited space."

My Epitaph

Instructions: How do you want others to remember you? Write a brief epitaph that would summarize your life. Use only the space on the front of the gravestone.

After a few minutes ask participants to get together in groups of three or four to share their epitaphs. Encourage individuals to talk with other people they don't know as well. This exchange with new friends will enlarge each person's caring community.

When groups have finished, say: "Most of us struggle with a personal sense of self-worth. This conflict may arise when we question our value or it may occur when we fail to understand that it's okay to use our positive self-esteem for our own benefit. No matter what struggle we face, conflicting feelings may cloud our eyes and minds to reality. If we don't feel good about ourselves, we won't be able to love others. We need to learn how to value ourselves and enjoy our own company."

EXPLORATION

(15 minutes) Ask the groups to turn to the "Rating Myself as a Friend" quiz. Tell them to read through the descriptions of friend-

ship. Have them take a few minutes to complete the quiz and think about their answers.

Rating Myself as a Friend

Instructions: Read through the following friendship descriptions. Choose the one that best describes you, or write your own description. Then complete the two open-ended statements at the end of the quiz.

My relationship with myself could be best described as:

The Love/Hate Friendship. I really like a few things about myself, but there are things about myself that I hate.

The Unmet Friendship. I don't know myself. I haven't the slightest idea who I am, and it's tough to love someone you don't know.

The Resentful Friendship. My relationship with myself is like one with a close relative that I wish I never had to visit.

The Ignored Friendship. I don't pay much attention to myself. Frankly, I don't concern myself with what it means to be my own best friend.

The Real Thing. I have a realistic view of my strengths and weaknesses. I can accept myself, forgive myself and love myself, all at the same time.

The _____ Friendship. (Come up with your own label and description.) _____

_____

1. I chose the label I did because _____

_____

2. To develop a real friendship with myself, I need_____

_____

_____

Say: "Share what you wrote with the rest of your small group. How did you describe yourself? Why did you choose that label? What do you need to do to be a better friend to yourself?"

If groups have trouble getting started, share your answers with the whole group. This kind of openness does three things:

● It sets the stage. If you can open up, so can they.

● It helps group members get to know you and establishes a relationship for the future.

● It illustrates the fact that you and the participants are in this together.

(10 minutes) After group members have had a few minutes to share their responses to the quiz, say: "Turn to 'A Realistic View of Myself.' Work alone for a couple of minutes to list your strengths and weaknesses. Label them according to the instructions at the top of the page."

A Realistic View of Myself ▬▬▬▬▬▬▬▬▬▬

Instructions: List your strengths and weaknesses.
- <u>Underline</u> the strengths you value the most.
- Draw a box around the strengths that can help you be a good friend to yourself.
- <u>Put a star</u> (★) beside those weaknesses you think you can change.
- Circle those weaknesses you need to accept.

Strengths	Weaknesses

After a few minutes ask two volunteers to read Romans 12:1-3 and 2 Corinthians 12:9-10. Then say: "Be realistic about yourself. Accept your strengths and weaknesses. Change what you can. Accept what you can't. Trust God to work through both your strengths and your weaknesses."

(15 minutes) Say: "Another critical link to self-esteem is self-discipline. Take care of yourself mentally, spiritually and physically. Develop habits that will work for you. Discipline yourself to know you are free to choose a certain behavior or a particular belief. Not to be disciplined is to feel captive to whatever pulls on you. Even though self-discipline contains an element of denial, freedom occurs as you make better choices with positive results.

"The words 'discipline' and 'disciple' come from the same root. When we discipline ourselves to follow Christ, we become his disciples. When we strive for what we want most and what is true, discipline becomes a positive choice. For example, it's easy to enjoy self-pity. There will always be someone more gifted, more attractive, more successful, more popular, more humorous or more 'whatever' than you.

"So, to feel good about yourself, you have to make a choice. Do you want the temporary comfort of self-pity, or do you prefer the certain security of knowing that God accepts you, has offered you special gifts and talents, and has great plans for your life? By rejecting self-pity and consciously choosing to think and say God's truth about yourself, your feelings will begin to change and you will realize you are valuable—you already are a special person!

"Turn to 'Tips to Being Your Own Best Friend.' Read the instructions at the top of the page and work alone to discover ways you can become even more valuable to yourself."

Tips to Being Your Own Best Friend ━━━━━━━━

Instructions: Read each of the following tips and complete the suggested activities.

Tip 1 **Give and receive forgiveness daily.** The Lord forgives you when you sin; you should do the same for others—and for *yourself*. When you fail to accept forgiveness, you may be overcome with guilt. When you fail to extend forgiveness, you can wipe yourself out with bitterness. Guilt and bitterness are enemies of a healthy self-esteem and the ability to love yourself. Human nature tends to rationalize or ignore sin. God tells us to name our sin and accept forgiveness.

"Blessed is he whose transgressions are forgiven, whose sins are covered. Blessed is the man whose sin the Lord does not count against him and in whose spirit is no deceit. When I kept silent, my bones wasted away through my groaning all day long. For day and night your hand was heavy upon me; my strength was sapped as in the heat of summer. Then I acknowledged my sin to you and did not cover up my iniquity. I said, 'I will confess my transgressions to the Lord'—and you forgave the guilt of my sin" (Psalm 32:1-5).

List your sins and accept God's forgiveness.

Tip 2 **Forgive resentments from the past.** Ask God to show you any resentments you have held from childhood.

Write a letter to God, outlining these resentments in detail. Turn the page sideways and write the words of 1 John 1:9 over the letter to symbolize how God can blot out these resentments from your life.

"If we confess our sins, he is faithful and just and will forgive us our sins and purify us from all unrighteousness" (1 John 1:9).

God,
    I have held on to these resentments from my childhood. Help me recognize and remove from my life the anger and frustration I feel from the following experiences:

Thank you for teaching me how to forgive.

_____
(Your name)

Tip 3 **Solve problems as quickly as possible.** Don't carry unresolved situations in your heart or your mind. Granted, not all problems can be solved quickly, but don't spend time brooding. If you choose to carry these unresolved issues, you will be preoccupied and your performance will deteriorate.

List those problems about which you are most concerned. Ask for God's guidance on how to solve these problems. Then brainstorm ideas for solving the problems you listed. Circle the ideas that feel best to you and act on at least one during the following week.

Tip 4 **Learn to enjoy your own company.** Take time to think about your-self, your likes and dislikes, your positive and negative qualities, the things you like to do and the things you like to talk about.

List several things you can enjoy doing alone. Plan to do at least one of these this week.

Tip 5 **Discover the difference between loneliness and aloneness through sharing solitude with God.** Jesus recognized the difference in these two states when he said to his disciples: "But a time is coming, and has come, when you will be scattered, each to his own home. You will leave me all alone. Yet I am not alone, for my Father is with me" (John 16:32).

Think about a time when you felt lonely. Perhaps your best friend chose to go somewhere with someone else instead of doing something with you. Next, recall a time when you spent some time alone with God. Maybe you were read-ing the Bible or watching a beautiful sunset. Describe the difference in your feelings in these situations.

Tip 6 **Laugh at yourself.** List things you've done that may seem strange to others. Maybe you used a word or term typical for your part of the country, but no one knew what you were talking about. List things you've done that seem funny to you. Perhaps you went on an important business trip and forgot all your shoes, except your tennis shoes. Think about how you looked to others and laugh out loud.

Write about one experience in which you can honestly laugh at yourself, and enjoy the fact that you sometimes do strange things.

Tip 7 **Accept your quirks as if you found them in your best friend.** You get used to your friend's strange or unusual ways of doing things. Soon you don't even notice because you thoroughly enjoy being with that person. Be as kind to yourself.

List those things about yourself that bother you or other people. Then take a look at your quirks realistically. Draw a line through the ones that probably can't be changed. Place an X over the ones that irritate you and no one else. Circle the ones you want to work on.

Tip 8 **Treat yourself as special as you treat your friends.** Think about how much fun it is to get a special gift for someone you like. Treat yourself as valuable and do the same for yourself.

Buy yourself a totally unpractical present this week. Tell one person what you bought for yourself, and celebrate the feeling of being special.

CLOSING

(5 minutes) As people begin to finish, ask them to meet again in their small groups to discuss these questions: "What other tips could you add to the list? Which tip seemed most valuable to you to help you become your own best friend?" After individuals have had a chance to share their thoughts and feelings, ask each person to pray

for the person on his or her left. Close by praying: "God, help all of us recognize our value as your creations. Work with each of us as we celebrate the excitement of being our own best friend. Amen."

Remind participants to take their Study Guides home, complete the "Solo" activity and bring them back to the next session. Let the members know the next study will deal with friendship. Encourage them to read Alan L. McGinnis' book *The Friendship Factor* (Augsburg).

Instructions: Place an X on each continuum to indicate the position that best represents you. Then answer the questions.

I would rather be:

Amazingly athletic	Unbelievably good-looking

◄ --- ►

Brilliant	Charming

◄ --- ►

Wealthy	Powerful

◄ --- ►

A very funny person	A very wise individual

◄ --- ►

Hard-working	Creative

◄ --- ►

Loved	Respected

◄ --- ►

Talented	Self-made

◄ --- ►

1. What has this survey told you about how society values you? _____
_____

2. What has this survey told you about how you value yourself? _____
_____

3. How can you use the results of this survey to help you be a better friend to yourself? _____
_____

Study 4

Friends

*F*riendships fortify our existence. Our lives diminish when friendships don't exist or fail to operate properly. But good friendships don't just happen. They take understanding and hard work.

Encourage the young adults in your group to think deeply about friendships. Why do people need friendships? What kinds of personal involvement and skills are required for friendships to exist and grow? Let participants know that this study will answer these questions and help them evaluate their role in this important relationship.

OBJECTIVES

In this study participants will:

● examine general principles for finding friends and establishing friendships.

● look at how God uses friendships to mold them into the people he wants them to be.

● discover how expectations affect relationships.
● continue to build a warm and caring support group of co-learners.

PREPARATION . . . .

☐ Study the material carefully and prayerfully.
☐ Gather markers, newsprint, pencils and Bibles.
☐ Contact four people before the meeting. Assign each person one of the friendships on the "Four Special Friendships" worksheet. Ask each person to read the material, summarize the relationship and draw some practical conclusions to share with the rest of the group.

OPENING

(5 minutes) Welcome everyone and introduce the session. Say: "For the past three weeks we have talked about the purpose of relationships, our relationship with our Creator and our relationship with ourselves. In this study we are going to reach beyond ourselves to those special people we call friends—the people with whom we talk, share, laugh and cry.

"To begin this study, think about your best friend when you were a child. What did you appreciate most about him or her? Was it a sense of humor? a willingness to cooperate? an ability to enjoy every moment? a capacity to find something exciting to do? Maybe you enjoyed the security of this person always being there for you, no matter what happened. Let's list some of the qualities you admired in your childhood friend." Write these ideas on a sheet of newsprint.

EXPLORATION

(15 minutes) After participants have had a chance to share, divide into small groups of four people. Ask the groups to turn to "Basic Questions About Friendship." Have individuals read the three questions, write their answers and discuss them within the small groups. Instruct them to appoint a leader who will report their group's findings to the total group. Give them five minutes to complete this activity.

Basic Questions About Friendship ▰▰▰▰▰▰▰▰

Instructions: Read the following questions and write your answers in the spaces provided. Discuss your answers within your small group.

1. How much does God care about whom I select as friends? Explain.

2. What are some of the methods I use to develop friendships?

3. What are some different levels of friendships and relationships?

Regroup and discuss one question at a time. Select one small group to begin the discussion on the first question, but encourage the other groups to add fresh information after the first group's spokesperson has completed the report. Choose a new group to start the discussion on the second question.

Answering the third question can be particularly creative and fun. List the friendship categories on newsprint as each group reports. Ask if anyone can think of other categories. Compare the lists to see whether any categories can be combined. Let participants know you will refer to this list later.

Explain to the group: "God didn't create you to be alone. In the first three studies, you found that God created you to have a relationship with him and with your fellow human beings. Everyone needs relationships. God uses friendship to meet your needs and help you become a stronger person.

"The book of Proverbs has much to say about relationships. 'As iron sharpens iron, so one man sharpens another' (Proverbs 27:17). God uses others to make you sharp, to make you more effective like a sharp knife or a sharp pair of scissors. 'He who walks with the wise grows wise, but a companion of fools suffers harm' (Proverbs 13:20). Your choice of friends can offer you a rich blessing or provide you with a serious problem.

"God provides all your relationships. A good way to find friends is to pray that God will bless you with the kind of individuals you need. God's in the business of meeting needs. Philippians 4:19 says, 'And my God will meet all your needs according to his glorious riches in Christ Jesus.' God wants to meet your needs for friendship, so talk to him about them.

"God sustains all relationships. It's difficult to have a proper perspective on relationships until you have a proper relationship with God. When you commit your life to Christ, you can deal more effectively with human relationships. When you realize that Christ has already paid the penalty for your sins and offer God control in your life, the Holy Spirit will work to transform you into a loving, understanding and forgiving person. You will become a better friend to others and to yourself because you have experienced a better relationship with God."

(10 minutes) Introduce the next activity by saying: "To illustrate how God works within relationships, let's look at some biblical examples of friendship. Turn to 'Four Special Friendships.' I've asked four people to briefly summarize these relationships for you." Encourage group members to listen carefully and take notes in the space provided in their Study Guides.

Four Special Friendships

Instructions: Listen carefully as group members share what they discovered about these friendships. As they mention the characteristics of each friendship, write notes in the space provided.

1. David and Jonathan. The friendship they shared is a great example of a love between two men who were willing to put each other above personal needs. (1 Samuel 18:1-4; 19:1-6; 20; 23:15-18)

 *Notes:*

2. Jesus, Mary, Martha and Lazarus. A tight bond existed among these four people. Grief, anger, support, availability and love were evident in this relationship. (Luke 10:38-42; John 11:1-7, 11-14, 17-44; 12:1-8)

▱▱▱▱⟶ *Notes:*

3. Paul and Barnabas. Barnabas was a great encourager. He believed in Paul, accepted him, introduced him to others and watched Paul become more famous than himself. With Mark, Barnabas again took a "loser" and helped him become the person God intended him to be. Barnabas probably taught Paul the deep meaning of friendships and throughout the epistles we see Paul's tight bond of friendships with others. (Acts 9:19b-21, 26-28; 11:25-26; 15:37-40; 2 Timothy 4:9-11)

▱▱▱▱⟶ *Notes:*

4. Jesus and the disciples, particularly Peter. Jesus spent most of his ministry with 12 men whom most considered cultural misfits. He accepted them and unconditionally loved them, even when they disappointed and deserted him. (Matthew 10:1-4, 34-39; 14:22-33; 26:40-46; Luke 6:40; John 18:15-27; 19:25-27)

▱▱▱▱⟶ *Notes:*

After the four group members have completed their presentations, ask participants to list some common characteristics of these four relationships. Characteristics to highlight might include the following:

● Consistency. These friendships were fairly reliable and long-lasting.

● Authenticity. These friendships were real; the friends seemed willing to share their true selves with each other.

● Unselfishness. Each friend noticed the other's needs and was concerned about the other's welfare.

● Tirelessness. With relentless determination, these friends worked on their relationships, despite difficulties.

(5 minutes) Say: "Earlier in this study, we listed several categories for friendships. Another way to categorize friendships is to describe the depth of each relationship. Some of your friendships are casual. You know the person's name and can make small talk. When you have common interests with someone and know some of his or her likes and dislikes, you might describe that person as an acquaintance. Good friends usually have shared something special and have spent time together, but golden friends are those individuals with whom you've shared most deeply. You've known each other for years, and both of you believe this friendship will endure and continue to grow."

Ask the group, "Why can't we be best friends with everyone?" After several people have responded, conclude this brief discussion with the following statement: "Even though some individuals strive to be everyone's best friend, they have to realize it's impossible to make this deep commitment to more than just a few people. No one has the time or the emotional energy to carry on a best-friend relationship with many people. To develop a deep friendship takes time, hard work, a willingness to risk and a desire to get close.

"Realize that friendships vary with the individuals and the relationship involved. Certain distinctions characterize our friendships with a marriage partner or our parents, an acquaintance or an intimate friend, an employer or an employee. It's important to understand each relationship we have and learn to accept its role in our lives.

"All of our friendships play an important role in developing the person God intends us to be. Each friendship is a part of the support and growth process we need to exist. But unrealistic expectations for any relationship can lead to anger and disappointment. Can you think of some positive or negative examples of how expectations can affect or have affected a relationship?"

(15 minutes) After participants have had a few moments to share, ask them to turn to the worksheet titled "Controlling My Expectations." Read the instructions and the example to make sure everyone knows what to do.

Controlling My Expectations ▬▬▬▬▬▬▬

Instructions: Read each Record of Disappointment and underline the individual's expectations. After you complete this section, read God's View and answer the questions at the end of that section.

Finally, rewrite the Records of Disappointment, eliminating the expectations. Create positive statements that celebrate the Flip Side of these negative experiences. (See the example.)

God's View:

"In the morning, O Lord, you hear my voice; in the morning I lay my requests before you and wait in expectation" (Psalm 5:3).

"For the kingdom of heaven is like a landowner who went out early in the morning to hire men to work in his vineyard. He agreed to pay them a denarius for the day and sent them into his vineyard.

"About the third hour he went out and saw others standing in the marketplace doing nothing. He told them, 'You also go and work in my

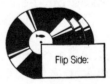

1. (Example)
I hate my job. Everyone's always in a hurry to get everything done. Individuals bicker among themselves to make sure I do their work first. I thought I'd be

1. (Example)
I have a unique opportunity to work with people who are hungry for others to care about them. I can illustrate God's love

working <u>as a</u>
<u>partner</u> with
these people to
complete this
project. It seems
no one notices
me, only the
work I do.

2. She was
my best friend. I
reached out to
her, brought her
into my group,
shared with her
and accepted
her as she was. I
was sure she
would do the
same for me, but
I guess I was
wrong.

3. He asked
me out several
times. I thought
our friendship
was special. We
could talk about
anything. But
then the phone
calls stopped.
I'm hurt, but he
doesn't seem to
notice my pain.

4. I came to
this church
group with high
expectations.
Everyone talked
about how
friendly the group
was. I got in-
volved and
shared what I
had to give, but
no one seemed
to notice. Now
I'm disappointed
and frustrated
with the group's
lack of response.

vineyard, and I will pay you whatever
is right.' So they went.

"He went out again about the
sixth hour and the ninth hour and did
the same thing. About the eleventh
hour he went out and found still others standing around. He asked them,
'Why have you been standing here
all day long doing nothing?'

' "Because no one has hired us,'
they answered.

"He said to them, 'You also go
and work in my vineyard.'

"When evening came, the owner
of the vineyard said to his foreman,
'Call the workers and pay them their
wages, beginning with the last ones
hired and going on to the first.'

"The workers who were hired
about the eleventh hour came and
each received a denarius. So when
those came who were hired first,
they expected to receive more. But
each one of them also received a
denarius. When they received it, they
began to grumble against the landowner. 'These men who were hired
last worked only one hour,' they said,
'and you have made them equal to
us who have borne the burden of the
work and the heat of the day.'

"But he answered one of them,
'Friend, I am not being unfair to you.
Didn't you agree to work for a denarius? Take your pay and go. I want to
give the man who was hired last the
same as I gave you. Don't I have the
right to do what I want with my own
money? Or are you envious because
I am generous?'

"So the last will be first, and the
first will be last" (Matthew 20:1-16).

"Therefore, as God's chosen
people, holy and dearly loved, clothe
yourselves with compassion, kindness, humility, gentleness and pa-
tience. Bear with each other and
forgive whatever grievances you may
have against one another. Forgive as
the Lord forgave you. And over all
these virtues put on love, which
binds them all together in perfect
unity.

with my pa-
tience and
kindness. I can
learn to listen
to their stress
and contribute
my calm to
help complete
this project.

2.

3.

4.

"Let the peace of Christ rule in your hearts, since as members of one body you were called to peace. And be thankful. Let the word of Christ dwell in you richly as you teach and admonish one another with all wisdom, and as you sing psalms, hymns and spiritual songs with gratitude in your hearts to God. And whatever you do, whether in word or deed, do it all in the name of the Lord Jesus, giving thanks to God the Father through him" (Colossians 3:12-17).

1. According to God's view, are expectations good or bad? Explain.___

_____
_____

2. How does God suggest you handle your expectations? _____

_____
_____

After everyone has completed the worksheet, ask participants to meet in small groups to discuss their answers. Then say: "Clarifying expectations often demands that you think realistically about a relationship and define the nature of that relationship. You may want to talk with that close friend or confidant to make sure you understand what you think or feel about the relationship. Or, in the case of a male-female relationship, you may want to discuss the nature of the relationship with the other person. *Be careful, however, that you don't spend more time thinking and talking about a relationship than you do living it.*"

CLOSING

(5 minutes) Say: "The key to finding friends is to be a friend. As you reach out to others, you will soon be surrounded by people who need you and want to be around you. Turn to 'To Be a Friend' and complete the self-evaluation. Take a look at yourself and focus on what it means to be a friend to others."

To Be a Friend

Instructions: Read the following suggestions on how to be a friend. Label each suggestion according to the following self-evaluation:

　　*—I do this; in fact, this is one of my best qualities.
　　S—I usually do this, but sometimes I forget or I just don't take the time.
　　W—I need to work on this one!
　　H—I find this extremely difficult. I may need some extra help in this area.

To be a friend I must:
　　_____ be willing to risk and be vulnerable with other people.
　　_____ be transparent and open.
　　_____ take off the mask I put on when I am around others.
　　_____ dare to be affectionate.
　　_____ do little or big things for other people.
　　_____ give my friends the freedom to expand and grow.
　　_____ accept others for who they are. I may not approve of what they do, but I can accept them.
　　_____ affirm others. I must look for the positive and help others accept the negative by sharing it in a positive way.
　　_____ learn to listen. I must approach others with the attitude, "Tell me more."
　　_____ talk and ask questions.
　　_____ be willing to forgive others when they let me down because no one is perfect, not even me!

Which of these suggestions is most important to me? _____
_____
How can I incorporate this suggestion into my life? _____
_____

Say: "Since we have acknowledged our valuable qualities and have realized where we need to grow, let's listen to some practical ways to begin this growth. Think about the following action plans and choose one as your project for the coming week." Read aloud each of the following suggestions:

● Pray about a personal friendship and your expectations for that relationship. Ask God to free you from your expectations and release both of you to enjoy the friendship and meet each other's needs.

● Select one friendship that you want to be special. Decide on something you want to do or say that will let the other person know how special he or she is to you.

● Make a sacrifice this week for someone else, but don't tell anyone about your sacrifice once it is done.

● Write an encouraging note to someone who has impacted your life. You may not have seen or heard from this individual in the last six months, so tell that person exactly what you appreciate about him or her.

Ask individuals to meet in pairs, share their choices with each other and close the session by praying for each other and the decisions that were made.

Explain the "Solo" assignment. Remind participants to bring their Study Guides back for the next study on the dating relationship. Encourage everyone to continue reading *The Friendship Factor*.

Instructions: Reach out to those people who have been special friends to you. Read each step and complete the suggested activity.

Step 1 Make a list of people or groups to whom you made phone calls during the past week. Add the names of others who are important to you. Include parents, close friends, church members, the people you work with and so on.

Step 2 Read the following situations. Think about who you would call in each situation and draw the appropriate symbol next to the names in Step 1.

 You need money, but you can't tell why.

 You feel depressed and need someone to cheer you up.

 You are struggling with a major decision at a crossroads in your life.

 It's 4 a.m. and you're in serious trouble. Who will get out of bed and come to your aid?

 You have a spiritual problem and need someone to listen, understand and possibly offer suggestions.

 You're flunking a correspondence course and need some help.

 You broke up with a romantic friend. Who will listen to your pain?

 You've got a great idea you'd like to put into practice, but you need help on a strategy.

Step 3 Respond to this open-ended statement:
From this exercise, I learned_____
_____

The Dating Relationship

Why do people choose to go through the dating experience? Is all of this relationship building really necessary? Why can't all individuals have an open and honest relationship with one another from the beginning?

This study will deal with the ideas and expectations participants have about relationships between men and women. It will provide a time for young adults to examine their attitudes about the opposite sex and what it takes to develop and maintain a quality relationship. Married couples will have the opportunity to reminisce about their experiences with their spouses and use this time to enrich the relationships they have chosen.

Encourage all participants to examine this transitional relationship carefully as they struggle with their choices for the future.

OBJECTIVES

In this study participants will:

● discuss the purposes of dating.
● look at ways to handle temptation in dating situations.
● learn how to end a dating relationship without destroying each other.
● brainstorm some creative dating ideas.
● continue to grow as a learning and caring community.

PREPARATION . . . .

☐ Study the material carefully and prayerfully.
☐ Gather newsprint, markers, masking tape, pencils and Bibles.

OPENING

(5 minutes) Welcome the group members and remind them that the emphasis for the last four studies has been on basic relationships, the kind individuals experience with God, themselves and others. The next three studies will go beyond the basics to concentrate on male-female relationships. These sessions will address the issues of dating, marriage and the single option.

To introduce this session, say: "Close your eyes and think about the perfect date. Where would you like to go? Would you go to the mountains? the beach? an elaborate houseboat? New York? the Caribbean? the Swiss Alps? Which location appeals to you most?" Give everyone a few moments to think.

Continue: "What would you want to do? Would you like to go skiing? take a cruise? see a famous play? attend a concert? spend the day away from the rest of the world? Be as creative and as extravagant as you wish. You may plan a leisurely breakfast in an elegant restaurant along the French Riviera. Or you might decide on a day of scuba diving and sailing off the coast of Hawaii. What would the ideal date be for you?" Pause to let people's minds begin to move.

After a couple of minutes tell everyone: "Now concentrate on the kind of date you have planned, and decide with whom you would like to share it. If you're single, you may want to share your perfect date with a favorite movie star or musician. Or you may be thinking about that special man or woman who lives nearby.

"If you're married, think about what you could do to let your spouse know this date is special because he or she is with you. Be creative. Think of some way you could make this time even more special for your spouse."

Ask participants to open their eyes and get together in pairs. If individuals are married, have them meet with their spouses. Say: "Take a moment to share your perfect date with your partner and explain why this date would be special for you. It's not necessary to share everything; a brief explanation will do."

Ask: "How many of you had similar ideas? How many of you liked the other person's idea better than your own? Why? How many of you planned a date you feel you could actually experience someday? How many of you dreamed the impossible?

"No matter what date you planned or with whom you planned to share it, each one of you had the opportunity to think about the dating relationship. This is not a new thought to any of you. Some of you may be experienced at the 'dating game,' while others may feel terribly uncomfortable even talking about it. Some of you have moved beyond the dating experience into marriage, but you still remember those feelings, experiences and expectations."

EXPLORATION

(10 minutes) After this introduction, divide participants into two groups: men and women. Give each group two sheets of newsprint and a marker. Have each group title one sheet of newsprint "What I Look for in My Friendships With People of the Opposite Sex." Have them title the other sheet "What I Look (or Looked) for in a Dating Relationship." Ask the groups to brainstorm ideas for each of these lists.

Then say: "After you've listed several traits under each statement, rank what you've written in order of importance. Give the most important trait a number one, the second most important trait a number two and so on. Obviously not everyone in your group will agree with the rankings, so use the majority's opinion."

Appoint a recorder and a timekeeper for each group. Remind both groups they will have five minutes to complete this activity.

Call the two groups back together. Have them tape their sheets of newsprint side by side so responses can be compared and contrasted. Ask the women to share what they look for in their friendships with men. Then ask the men to share what they look for in their friendships with women. Ask: "How are the lists alike? different?" Discuss people's responses.

Have the men share what they look for in a dating relationship. Then have the women share what they look for. Discuss the comparisons and the contrasts. Keep the discussion light and fun, but highlight the differences.

(5 minutes) At this point ask participants: "Why do you date? What are some of the purposes for dating?" List responses on newsprint. As participants add to the list, make sure they include the following ideas:

● Dating enhances social skills. It provides a testing ground for learning how to meet and relate with different types of people.

● Dating teaches you about yourself. Within a dating relationship, strengths and weaknesses are exposed and growth can occur.

● Dating provides an opportunity to observe different traits and personalities. It helps a person decide what he or she wants or doesn't want in a marriage partner.

● Dating is the way our culture handles courtship. No longer do parents arrange marriages nor do barbarians swoop in from the East to ride off with a wife. Dating is the process people go through to determine whom they are going to marry. Marriage is usually preceded by dating. So if you want to get married, you'll probably need to date.

Continue this discussion by asking, "Are there any particular reasons why people shouldn't date?" Allow participants to contribute their own ideas, but be sure to include the following:

● If a person realizes that his or her life goals have priority over relationships, he or she may want to delay or forgo the dating experience.

● If someone has been deeply hurt in a relationship, he or she may need time to heal.

● If someone has been sexually involved, he or she may need time to regain personal strength and heal spiritually before entering the dating scene again.

Say to the group: "Let's look at the dating experience from a Christian perspective. Why should Christians date? Should their purposes be any different? Why or why not? Are there reasons Christians shouldn't date? Does being Christian make a difference in the dating experience?" List responses on a sheet of newsprint. Issues you may want to address include the following:

● The Bible is silent on the subject of dating because the culture 2,000 years ago didn't have the same type of courtship. But God's Word is not silent on the type of people with whom we are to relate. "Do not be yoked together with unbelievers. For what do righteousness and wickedness have in common? Or what fellowship can light have with darkness? . . . What does a believer have in common with an unbeliever? What agreement is there between the temple of God and idols? For we are the temple of the living God. As God has said: 'I will live with them and walk among them, and I will be their God, and they will be my people' "(2 Corinthians 6:14-16).

● When Christian men delay or neglect dating, Christian women may not receive many invitations and may feel compelled to date non-Christian men. Discuss this situation from both perspectives. Encourage participants to develop alternatives for both men and women.

● If individuals feel God is calling them to a specific task, they may find it unwise to get involved. For instance, if a person is committed to a two-year mission project and must leave in a month, a dating relationship may not be appropriate.

● Christians need to be cautious about using their spiritual commitment as an excuse not to date, especially if they have plans for a spouse and family in the future.

(5 minutes) After this discussion, divide participants into groups of four. Tell the groups: "We've dealt with generalities and theories; now it's time to work on practical matters. Each group will prepare a role play based on one of the following suggestions." Give each group one of the following situations:

● How not to ask for a date.

● How to ask someone out properly.

● How a woman can comfortably ask a man to go out.

Allow three minutes to prepare. Then ask each group to present its role play to the other groups.

(10 minutes) Say: "Keep your same small groups, and let's examine two crucial aspects of the dating relationship—sexual temptation and breaking up. Almost every couple who dates for an extended period of time is tempted sexually. To ignore this temptation is to be unprepared. To say this experience could never happen to you is naive. To believe that God alone will control your response in this situation is to negate one of his greatest creations—the human mind.

"Turn to 'Sex: A Temptation With a Choice.' Answer the questions on this worksheet and discuss this important issue with the people in your small group."

Sex: A Temptation With a Choice ▰▰▰▰▰▰

Instructions: Read the following suggestions and answer the questions. Discuss your answers within your small group. Use this time to listen and learn from others about how they have handled sexual temptation.

1. Give yourself as much credit as God does. "No temptation has seized you except what is common to man. And God is faithful; he will not let you be tempted beyond what you can bear. But when you are tempted, he will also provide a way out so that you can stand up under it" (1 Corinthians 10:13).

What "way out" will God provide when you are sexually tempted? Is this some kind of magic trick, or how does God provide this kind of help? Explain your answer.

2. Accept the fact that you have sexual feelings, and deal with them ahead of time. Sexual immorality usually begins in the mind. Thoughts lead to desire, and desire leads to action. "When tempted, no one should say, 'God is tempting me.' For God cannot be tempted by evil, nor does he tempt anyone; but each one is tempted when, by his own evil desire, he is dragged away and enticed" (James 1:13-14).

What can you do to control your sexual feelings? How can you handle the sexual thoughts and images that enter your mind?

3. Recognize your weaknesses and ask for help. If you're struggling in this area, confess it to a friend. Ask that friend to listen to you and help you be accountable for what you will do on a date. Talk about where to go, what to do and how to handle those unplanned moments. "For the foolishness of God is wiser than man's wisdom, and the weakness of God is stronger than man's strength" (1 Corinthians 1:25).

How can God's wisdom and strength provide you with additional support?

4. Avoid putting yourself in dating situations in which you know you can lose control. The two of you alone in your apartment may not be the best place to fight sexual temptation. Dating men or women whose standards are different from your own can cloud your decisions. "Be very careful, then, how you live—not as unwise but as wise . . ." (Ephesians 5:15).

What kinds of people should you avoid? What places would be off-limits? Which activities are inappropriate for you?

5. In the midst of temptation, choose to walk (or run!) away from the situation. Read Joseph's story in Genesis 39. Unlike the story of David and Bathsheba in 2 Samuel 11, Joseph avoided continual temptation because of loyalty to his master and to God. When the situation became too intense, Joseph chose to walk away.

Choosing to move away from each other in the midst of intense feelings isn't easy. It requires tremendous personal strength. But the Bible assures you that you can handle these intense feelings. "I can do everything through him who gives me strength" (Philippians 4:13).

How can you and your dating partner learn to handle this intensity? What specific strengths can you use?

6. Realize that if you make a poor choice, life isn't over. The choice may have felt good at the moment, but guilt and the fear that it may happen again can rob your relationship of opportunities for growth.

Remember, God forgives. "If we confess our sins, he is faithful and just and will forgive us our sins and purify us from all unrighteousness" (1 John 1:9). But how can you forgive yourself? "Therefore, if anyone is in Christ, he is a new creation; the old has gone, the new has come!" (2 Corinthians 5:17). How can these words provide the healing strength you need?

(10 minutes) Recognize that most groups won't be through with their discussions, but encourage them to continue these conversations later. Let them know you need to move on to another important aspect of dating.

Say: "Breaking up is one of the most difficult tasks in a dating relationship. Done properly with God's direction, guidance and peace, breaking up can bring relief and also encourage positive steps toward future relationships. Done improperly, breaking up can destroy people or plant seeds of mistrust and bitterness that can last for years.

"Within your small group, brainstorm some creative ideas on how to break up and maintain each person's integrity. Some of you may have had this experience. Others of you may have listened to a friend and worked with him or her to overcome this experience. Share your concerns and ideas with the rest of your group."

After a few minutes, ask participants to share their ideas on how to break up. List these ideas on a sheet of newsprint. Then have everyone turn to "Breaking Up: An Opportunity or a Disaster?" Ask participants to read the suggestions and respond to the questions at the end.

Breaking Up: An Opportunity or a Disaster? ▬▬▬

Instructions: Read these suggestions and answer the questions.

1. Maintain proper communication throughout a dating relationship. When both parties communicate well in the beginning, expectation levels are more realistic. The initial feelings of romance make communication difficult. Carelessly chosen words can raise expectations unrealistically and, frankly, untruthfully. So be careful about what you say and promise.

2. Be cautious physically. Physical communication can say just as much as words. Stay aware of what your actions are saying. Don't get overly involved. This personal awareness prevents much guilt and bitterness if a breakup does occur.

3. Maintain a good friendship within the dating relationship. Since doing things together and communicating are part of all relationships, you can rebuild a friendship on the special conversations and experiences that were meaningful to both of you before you broke up.

4. During the process of breaking up, communicate carefully and precisely.

Talk about appropriate concerns, but don't pick on every little fault. Share some of the highlights and positive parts of the relationship rather than focus on the negative aspects.

Try to be realistic about yourself. Obviously, you aren't perfect. Try to learn something about yourself during the process of breaking up just as you did during the course of the relationship.

Listen to the other person, and don't argue. Rarely can you convince someone you're right, especially when feelings are involved.

5. Be realistic about your dating relationships. Each one will ultimately break up or lead to marriage. Breaking up can be a learning experience or a disaster. Allow God to use breakups to teach you about yourself and others. That's part of the risk and part of the beauty of dating relationships.

6. Have faith in God's involvement in your life. Recognize God's strength to help you recover and learn from a painful experience. Believe in God's steadfastness to provide you with what you need. Have confidence in God's truth to relieve your anxiety, depression and frustration. "And we know that in all things God works for the good of those who love him, who have been called according to his purpose" (Romans 8:28).

a. Which of these suggestions is most meaningful to you? Why? _____
_____
b. What other suggestions would you add to this list? _____
_____

(5 minutes) Say: "Let's conclude this study with a fun activity. During the next two minutes, meet with four other people to talk about creative ideas for dating. Try to list at least five fun things you can do on a date." Tape a sheet of newsprint on the wall while the groups are talking. Title it "Creative Dating Ideas." After two minutes, ask group members to share their lists. Write all ideas on the newsprint. Try to come up with a list of at least 20 ideas.

CLOSING

(5 minutes) Have participants stay in their small groups. Ask each person to decide which part of this study was most meaningful to him or her and share why with the rest of the small group.

Close with the following prayer: "God, all of us strive to be special to someone. Use us in all of our relationships as agents of your love. May our interactions with others reflect the fact that we are special to you. In Christ's name we pray, amen."

Explain that the "Solo" activity for this study will use the list of creative dating ideas. Ask participants to write these ideas in the "Solo" activity in their Study Guides. Remind participants to bring their Study Guides back to the next session. Encourage everyone to read *Creative Dating* by Doug Fields and Todd Temple (Oliver-Nelson).

Let the group know that the next study will concentrate on the marriage relationship.

Solo ━━━━━━━━━━━━━━━━━━━━━━━━━

Instructions: Choose one of the creative dating ideas suggested during this study or create one of your own. Develop the idea by making all the plans and arrangements, and invite someone to share it with you.

◆◆◆◆◆◆◆◆◆◆◆◆◆◆◆ **Creative Dating Ideas** ◆◆◆◆◆◆◆◆◆◆◆◆◆◆◆

If you are a man and have been reluctant to date in the past, plan to double-date with a friend or participate in some co-ed activity or sport in which you feel comfortable.

If you are a woman and feel uncomfortable about asking a guy for a date, plan a party or an event (dinner, picnic, etc.) to include several of your friends, both men and women.

If you are married, schedule a special date with your spouse. Talk about your dating memories and take time out to get reacquainted as friends.

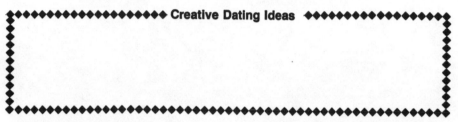

My Dating Plan

What will we do?

Where?

When?

With whom?

Marriage: God's Good Idea

*D*o I really want to get married? What expectations do I have for marriage? Is marriage really as wonderful or as terrible as others say it is?

The concept of marriage stirs up a variety of questions and emotions. Most people long to marry someday, but many are reluctant for a variety of reasons. Some have other things they want to do first. Others come from homes where marriage more closely resembles war than love. Some don't feel mature enough to enter a marriage commitment. And others aren't sure they would choose that option, even if it were available.

This study is designed to bring participants' fears into the open. It seeks to paint a realistic picture of two imperfect individuals helping each other become more than they could be alone. It points out that if people decide to marry, they marry both a sinner and a child of God.

Help group members deal with this unique relationship. Be open and honest with them. If you are married, talk about your own relationship. If you aren't married, talk about your own dreams and fears regarding marriage. Since sex is an integral part of marriage and plays a key role in the courtship process, be prepared to talk openly about this subject and the power it has in the male-female relationship. Your willingness to discuss this topic will strengthen the learning process for your group members.

Discussing marriage and sex with a group of young adults is a challenging task. Encourage your young adults to enter the study with open minds and a willingness to learn. Let them know you will work with them as they search for answers to their questions and solutions to their concerns. Reassure them that God's presence will help them accept and love one another as they struggle together.

OBJECTIVES

In this study participants will:

● discover characteristics of a good marriage by looking at both good and poor marriages.

● talk about the kind of person they are looking for in a marriage relationship.

● discuss God's intentions for marriage.

● examine the roles God has for husbands and wives.

● talk about God's view of sex within the marriage relationship.

● continue to build a learning and caring community.

PREPARATION . . . .

☐ Study the material carefully and prayerfully.
☐ Gather newsprint, markers, masking tape, pencils and Bibles.

OPENING

(5 minutes) Say: "During the first four studies, we looked at basic relationships. In the last study, we talked about dating relationships. This study will examine the unique relationship of marriage."

Have participants turn to "Why Someone Should Marry Me." Ask individuals to write a 30-second commercial on why someone should marry them. Ask them to think about what personal characteristics would make them an excellent mate and why people should take advantage of this opportunity to tie the matrimonial knot. Let them know the commercial can be humorous or serious, but it should contain an element of truth.

Why Someone Should Marry Me

 Instructions: Write a 30-second commercial message to persuade someone to marry you. Use humor or keep your message serious, but be truthful. Be prepared to share your message in a small group.

Divide into small groups of four people. Ask participants to share their commercials with the rest of their group.

EXPLORATION

(10 minutes) Give each small group a sheet of newsprint and a marker. Have each group appoint a recorder. Ask recorders to divide their newsprint in half by drawing a line from top to bottom. On the left side, have them write the word "Good"; on the right side, the word "Bad."

Ask individuals to talk briefly about one of the best marriages they've ever seen. As they speak, have group members listen for the characteristics of a good marriage and help the recorder write them on the newsprint. For instance, a person might say, "The thing I liked most about Bob and Traci's marriage was how well they communicated, even on tough issues, without becoming angry." Then the recorder might write the words "good communication" and "anger management" under the word "Good."

After a few minutes, have group members talk about the poorest marriages they've seen. Ask participants not to mention names, but to describe some unhealthy marital characteristics they've noticed. Have recorders list these characteristics under the word "Bad." Have all groups tape their lists on the wall. Read the good characteristics first, then read the bad. Draw a line through duplicate characteristics to make lists more readable. Leave lists taped to the wall as the study continues.

(15 minutes) Have participants turn to the "Flexibility Checklist." Say: "Each of you has expectations that a marriage partner must meet. Obviously some of these factors may be more important to you than others. Take a few minutes to complete the 'Flexibility Checklist.' "

Flexibility Checklist ▬▬▬▬▬▬▬▬▬▬

Instructions: Circle a number from 1 to 5 for each of the following factors according to its importance to you (1 = don't care; 5 = absolutely necessary). The numbers in between indicate these factors are negotiable.

How important is it to you that your mate:

Don't care		Absolutely necessary			
1	2	3	4	5	Attends church
1	2	3	4	5	Is a mature Christian
1	2	3	4	5	Is a member of your denomination
1	2	3	4	5	Is a high school graduate
1	2	3	4	5	Is a college graduate
1	2	3	4	5	Likes the same kind of food you do
1	2	3	4	5	Has good table manners
1	2	3	4	5	Agrees with your attitudes toward sex
1	2	3	4	5	Gets along well with your family
1	2	3	4	5	Agrees with you about having children
1	2	3	4	5	Agrees with you about your respective roles in the home
1	2	3	4	5	Is comfortable with your friends
1	2	3	4	5	Is a good host or hostess
1	2	3	4	5	Laughs at the same jokes you do
1	2	3	4	5	Is punctual
1	2	3	4	5	Agrees with you about buying on credit or paying cash
1	2	3	4	5	Will watch football games with you
1	2	3	4	5	Will attend a classical music concert with you
1	2	3	4	5	Knows how to resolve conflicts peacefully
1	2	3	4	5	Is in the habit of tithing
1	2	3	4	5	Agrees with you about talking about the past
1	2	3	4	5	Is articulate
1	2	3	4	5	Is physically attractive
1	2	3	4	5	Is an orderly person
1	2	3	4	5	Is a thinker
1	2	3	4	5	Is outgoing
1	2	3	4	5	Can cook
1	2	3	4	5	Has proven that he or she can hold a job
1	2	3	4	5	Would be a good mother or father
1	2	3	4	5	Consistently brings out the best in you
1	2	3	4	5	Is a virgin

Grade Your Flexibility:

If you have all 5s, you're probably a deluded dreamer or a confirmed celibate. If you have all 1s, spend some time thinking realistically about these factors and how they could affect a marriage relationship.

When participants complete their checklists, ask them to think about how flexible they are. Say: "Look at the factors where you circled a 1 or a 5. Think about what you expect from a marriage partner. Now think about those same factors for yourself. Do you expect more from others than you do from yourself? Select those areas on which you need to work at being more flexible."

(20 minutes) Have participants stay in their small groups. Ask them to turn to "A Biblical View of Marriage." Introduce the next activity: "Many times we assume that spouses should live up to our role expectations before they consider their own. The Bible explains various expectations and roles for marriage. As you discuss the following questions, remember you don't have to agree, but you do need to listen, respect each other's opinions and learn from each other."

A Biblical View of Marriage

Instructions: Read the scripture passages and answer the questions that follow. Discuss these questions in your small group.

God's Intentions for Marriage:

"Then God said, 'Let us make man in our image, in our likeness, and let them rule over the fish of the sea and the birds of the air, over the livestock, over all the earth, and over all the creatures that move along the ground.'

"So God created man in his own image, in the image of God he created him; male and female he created them.

"God blessed them and said to them, 'Be fruitful and increase in number; fill the earth and subdue it. Rule over the fish of the sea and the birds of the air and over every living creature that moves on the ground' " (Genesis 1:26-28).

"The Lord God took the man and put him in the Garden of Eden to work it and take care of it . . . The Lord God said, 'It is not good for the man to be alone. I will make a helper suitable for him.'

"Now the Lord God had formed out of the ground all the beasts of the field and all the birds of the air . . . But for Adam no suitable helper was found. So the Lord God caused the man to fall into a deep sleep; and while he was sleeping, he took one of the man's ribs and closed up the place with flesh. Then the Lord God made a woman from the rib he had taken out of the man, and he brought her to the man.

"The man said, 'This is now bone of my bones and flesh of my flesh; she shall be called "woman," for she was taken out of man.'

"For this reason a man will leave his father and mother and be united to his wife, and they will become one flesh" (Genesis 2:15, 18-24).

1. What do you think God had in mind when he brought men and women together in marriage?

2. List the specific intentions for marriage mentioned in the Genesis passages you just read.

Paul's Directions for Husbands and Wives:

"Submit to one another out of reverence for Christ.

"Wives, submit to your husbands as to the Lord. For the husband is the head of the wife as Christ is the head of the church . . . Now as the church submits to Christ, so also wives should submit to their husbands in everything.

"Husbands, love your wives, just as Christ loved the church and gave himself up for her to make her holy . . . In this same way, husbands ought to love their wives as their own bodies. He who loves his wife loves himself. After all, no one ever hated his own body, but he feeds and cares for it, just as Christ does the church . . . each one of you also must love his wife as he loves himself, and the wife must respect her husband" (Ephesians 5:21-26, 28-29, 33).

This scripture passage was written by the Apostle Paul almost 2,000 years ago. Even though this passage sometimes leads to controversy, discuss it with an open mind and a willingness to learn.

1. What basic principle for a relationship does Paul recommend for both husbands and wives? Why?

2. How should wives treat their husbands? Why?

3. How should husbands treat their wives? Explain the role model Paul uses to describe this relationship.

4. What principle of love does Paul recommend for the marriage relationship?

5. If Paul were alive today, what questions would you ask to clarify your understanding of these verses?

6. How does the first sentence bring perspective to the rest of this passage?

Sexuality—A Part of the Total Package:

"The truth is that wherever a man lies with a woman, there, whether they like it or not, a transcendental relation is set up between them which must be eternally enjoyed or eternally endured."—C.S. Lewis, *The Screwtape Letters* (Revell).

"Do you not know that your bodies are members of Christ himself? Shall I then take the members of Christ and unite them with a prostitute? Never! Do you not know that he who unites himself with a prostitute is one with her in body? For it is said, 'The two will become one flesh' . . . Flee from sexual immorality. All other sins a man commits are outside his body, but he who sins sexually sins against his own body" (1 Corinthians 6:15-16, 18).

1. How do the quotation and scripture passages relate to the marriage relationship?

2. How is sexual immorality different from other sins?

A New Way to Relate:
"Love is patient, love is kind. It does not envy, it does not boast, it is not proud. It is not rude, it is not self-seeking, it is not easily angered, it keeps no record of wrongs. Love does not delight in evil but rejoices with the truth. It always protects, always trusts, always hopes, always perseveres" (1 Corinthians 13:4-7).

This love chapter offers specific directions for a successful marriage relationship that will last. Examine your relationship in light of these directions to see if it can become the unique relationship promised by God.

Call the small groups back together and ask: "What did you discover about marriage in the Bible passages you just read? What questions do you still have?" Use the following questions to stimulate further discussion if you have time:

1. How can marriage help two individuals "complete" each other?

2. What is the importance of intimacy and companionship within a relationship?

3. Why does God include the responsibility of procreation within marriage?

4. Why did God design the task of having dominion as a partnership?

5. How can marriage help individuals understand the relationship of God to his people?

After a brief discussion say: "In 2 Corinthians 6:14, Paul cautions you not to be yoked with unbelievers. He realized that when your relationship with Christ is the most important aspect of your life, it is difficult to share intimacy and companionship with a partner whose priority is not the same. Even raising children can be difficult if parents don't share this deepest commitment in their lives. God desires the best for you, and marrying an unbeliever would not be best.

"Recognize the fact that when you marry, you marry a child of God, but you also marry a sinner. Marrying a Christian doesn't mean life will be easy or there will be no disappointments. Look for spiritual maturity in the person you choose to marry, but regardless of how spiritually mature that person is, realize he or she will still disappoint you at times. That's why marriage will never take the place of a relationship with Christ, the one relationship that never fails.

"Instead of concentrating on *finding* the right person, concentrate on *being* the right person. In areas of weakness, ask God to mold you into a stronger person. In areas of strength, ask the Lord to continue to develop those traits."

CLOSING

(5 minutes) Say: "During this study you've had a chance to think about yourself and your ideas about marriage. You've examined God's ideas about this special relationship, and you've had a chance to think about whether this kind of relationship is meant for you."

Close the meeting with the following prayer: "God, we recognize the marriage relationship as one of your most valuable creations. Help us realize where we need to grow personally. Use us as your instruments to accept those we love as they are. Give us the strength we need to make the lifetime decisions that glorify this unique relationship. In the name of him who blessed this relationship with his first miracle, our Lord Jesus Christ, amen."

Instruct group members to complete the "Solo" activity and bring their Study Guides back to the next study, which is on singleness. Encourage them to read *As for Me and My House* by Walter Wangerin (Thomas Nelson).

Instructions: Interview two or three couples whose marriages you admire. Or talk with a widow or widower who had a good marriage. Ask each person the following questions:

 1. What is the secret of your marriage's success?
 2. What unexpected surprises in your spouse did you encounter *after* you were married?
 3. What important changes did you make after your marriage began? Why?
 4. What important changes did your spouse make after your marriage began? Why?

Through these conversations, my views about marriage have changed or remained the same in the following ways:

Study 7

The Single Option

*N*ot everyone will marry. Many will remain single. Some will marry and then through death or divorce suddenly will become single again, sometimes for the rest of their lives. After examining marriage through God's eyes, it is wise to look at singleness in the same way. Encourage your young adults to appreciate the life situations in which they find themselves and live abundantly with Christ whether they are married or single.

OBJECTIVES

In this study participants will:
- help other group members appreciate the situation in which they find themselves.
- understand the factors that lead to extended singleness.
- develop a set of principles for living abundantly as a single person.

- develop a set of principles that will allow individuals to celebrate their individuality within marriage.
- continue to develop a warm and caring learning community.

PREPARATION . . . .

☐ Study the material carefully and prayerfully.
☐ Gather newsprint, markers, pencils and Bibles.

OPENING

(5 minutes) Introduce this study by saying: "After talking about relationships and marriage, our focus now shifts to the single life. Complete this statement in your own words: 'If I were single for the rest of my life, I would . . .' You might say how you would feel or what you would like to accomplish. Create your own response to this open-ended statement."

Have individuals get together in groups of two to share their responses. Make sure everyone has a partner. Have participants listen carefully so they can share the other person's response with the rest of the group.

EXPLORATION

(15 minutes) After everyone has had a chance to share, start this study by dividing participants into two groups. Give one group responsibility for building a case for marriage. Give the other group responsibility for building a case for the single life. Allow groups 10 minutes to develop their cases and prepare their presentations. They can use a humorous skit, a role play, a debate or any other method of presentation they want.

After each group presents its case, list the major points on newsprint. After both presentations, examine the lists to see which presentation seems most convincing. These informal presentations and the discussion should provide humor and warmth as group members begin to think through the single option.

(5 minutes) Say: "People in our society are waiting longer to marry than they have in the past. Some have chosen not to pursue this relationship at all. Consequently, there are more single young people than ever before. Why are people waiting? Why are people deciding against marriage?" Encourage your young adults to offer their own ideas. Be sure to include the following points:

● Fear and hesitancy. More and more young adults have grown up in homes where divorce has been a factor. Seeing their parents separate and living in a single-parent home have contributed to some hesitancy regarding marriage. Young people are afraid of seeing their own marriage dissolve. And because they lack confidence in their ability to make marriage work, they hesitate. Then they look for "the perfect mate"—but finding perfection takes a long time!

● Career pursuit. Society's emphasis on developing a career has pushed marriage down the priority list, especially for women. Today's young women are encouraged to join the work force, to become professionals, to begin a career. This career emphasis has made early marriages less appealing.

● Cultural norm. Because there are more single people, the predominant message today is, "It's okay to be single." Organizations and churches offer more singles groups and activities, so there are more options for single people.

● Time to check out the options. To delay this major decision means more time to evaluate what you really want. Does marriage fit for you, or is this an option you want to eliminate from your life? If marriage is your choice, what do you want in a mate? How can marriage help you fulfill your dreams and plans for the future?

● Freedom from responsibility. Many people don't want the responsibilities that come with marriage. They appreciate the freedom they have and see little reason to alter their lifestyle. The addition of a spouse and the possibility of children seem to eliminate the spontaneity and the freedom they feel with the single life.

(20 minutes) Conclude this discussion by saying: "Since more and more people remain single and since many who marry have the potential to be single again, let's talk about a positive perspective on singleness and some helps for living the single life. In addition to this concentration on being single, we'll consider how to maintain our singleness, or individuality, within marriage.

"If you are single, turn to 'Living Abundantly as a Single.' If you are married, turn to 'Recognizing Your Individuality Within Marriage.' Both of these worksheets deal with the same ideas, but the content and questions have been altered slightly to make discussions more relative to your situation. Complete this activity alone in keeping with our theme of being single."

Living Abundantly as a Single ▬▬▬▬▬▬▬

Instructions: Read each suggestion and answer the questions that follow.

1. Be realistic about marriage. For most people marriage is a good part of God's overall plan, but marriage isn't always the ultimate experience, the fulfillment of life or the pinnacle of relationships. Marriage doesn't always solve problems; sometimes it creates them.
   a. Do I glorify marriage, or do I look at it realistically? Explain.

   b. How does marriage fit into my plans for life?

2. Use your singleness as an opportunity to learn. God doesn't waste any experiences. He may want you single while he teaches you some important lessons. He may also want you single so you can devote large chunks of time to some great ministry he has for you. Use your singleness to learn what God has to teach you.
   a. What have I learned from being single?

   b. How has God used my singleness to help me grow as an individual?

   c. How have I used my singleness to develop new personal strengths?

3. Enjoy your singleness. Learn to relax and have fun with friends of both sexes. Desperate attempts to date and the frantic pursuit of marriage tend to push people away.
   a. What do I enjoy about being single?

   b. List both male and female friends. Which of these people would continue to be friends even if I were married? Which would not? Why?

4. Accept who you are. Being single is not second-class citizenship. God's promises aren't based on who's married and who's not. "The Lord delights in those who fear him, who put their hope in his unfailing love" (Psalm 147:11). "No good thing does he withhold from those whose walk is blameless" (Psalm 84:11b). God's promises apply to everyone, not just married people.
   a. What do I like best about who I am right now?

   b. How can God use me as I am?

5. Be thankful for the life and opportunities you have. "Do not be anxious about anything, but in everything, by prayer and petition, with thanksgiving, present your requests to God. And the peace of God, which transcends all understanding, will guard your hearts and your minds in Christ Jesus" (Philippians 4:6-7). Being thankful produces a positive spirit. When you share your positive spirit with others, not only are you blessed, but you bless others.
   a. For what part of my life am I most thankful?

   b. How can I share a positive spirit with others?

6. Accept your sexuality, but subject it to Christ. Don't deny your maleness or your femaleness. Some people deny their sexuality as an attempt to remain morally pure. This denial leaves a huge hole in their personality. Accept the fact that God created you as a sexual being. Celebrate your femininity or your masculinity as part of God's creation.

a. What does it mean to accept my femininity or my masculinity?

b. How can I celebrate this part of my life as a single who is morally responsible to his or her Creator? Be specific.

7. Live life creatively. Dive into a variety of interests and develop your talents and gifts. As a married person, you may not have time to develop these special interests. Don't live life waiting for something to happen. Trust that God knows you and can put together the big and little details of your life.

a. What special interests can I pursue right now?

b. How can I use this time in my life to fulfill personal interests and goals?

8. Walk by faith. "Now faith is being sure of what we hope for and certain of what we do not see . . . And without faith it is impossible to please God, because anyone who comes to him must believe that he exists and that he rewards those who earnestly seek him" (Hebrews 11:1, 6). Besides the truths that God will bless you and walk beside you, there are no guarantees in life. No one knows for sure whether he or she will marry, have children, get the job he or she wants, or make the cover of TIME Magazine. Walk step by step, one day at a time.

a. How can I walk by faith?

b. In what specific areas of my life do I need to take the first step of faith?

9. Don't make your singleness an art form. It's fine to be single, but don't wave your singleness like a banner in other people's faces. Be open to the possibility of marriage. Don't shut off yourself or God from this possibility.

How can I celebrate my singleness without offending others?

Recognizing Your Individuality Within Marriage

Instructions: Read each suggestion and answer the questions that follow.

1. Be realistic about marriage. For most people marriage is a good part of God's overall plan, but marriage isn't always the ultimate experience, the fulfillment of life or the pinnacle of relationships. Marriage doesn't always solve problems; sometimes it creates them.

a. Do I glorify marriage, or do I look at it realistically? Explain.

b. How can I maintain my individuality within my marriage relationship?

2. Use your marriage as an opportunity to learn. God doesn't waste any experiences. He may use your marriage to teach you some important lessons about yourself and your spouse. He may use your marriage to teach you how to work closely with another person to serve God. Use your marriage as a place to grow as an individual.

a. What have I learned about myself from being married?

b. How has God used my marriage to help me grow as an individual?

c. How have I used my marriage to develop new personal strengths?

3. Enjoy yourself within the marriage relationship. Relax and have fun with your spouse. Learn to appreciate each other's friends. By sharing these moments, you will maintain that joyful quality that attracted you to each other as you began your relationship.

a. What part of your marriage do you enjoy most?

b. List your closest friends. Which friends are yours alone? Which friends primarily belong to your spouse? Which friends do you mutually enjoy?

c. How can you learn to appreciate all your friends?

4. Accept who you are. Being married doesn't limit your relationship with God and his world. "The Lord delights in those who fear him, who put their hope in his unfailing love" (Psalm 147:11). "No good thing does he withhold from those whose walk is blameless" (Psalm 84:11b). God's promises apply to each person.

a. What do I like best about who I am right now?

b. How can God use me as I am?

5. Be thankful for the life and opportunities you have. "Do not be anxious about anything, but in everything, by prayer and petition, with thanksgiving, present your requests to God. And the peace of God, which transcends all understanding, will guard your hearts and your minds in Christ Jesus" (Philippians 4:6-7). Being thankful produces a positive spirit. When you share your positive spirit with others, not only are you blessed, but you bless others.

a. For what part of my life am I most thankful?

b. How can I share a positive spirit with others?

6. Accept your sexuality, and subject it to Christ. The physical relationship is a vital part of any marriage. So accept yourself and the sexuality of your spouse. Celebrate your femininity or masculinity as part of God's creation. Use this special gift to enhance your relationship with each other.

a. What does it mean to accept my sexuality?

b. How can I celebrate my femininity or my masculinity in a way that glorifies Christ and enhances my marriage relationship?

7. Live life creatively. Accept the fact that you are an individual with your own interests and ideas. Develop your talents and gifts. Make it a priority to give time and energy to your relationship with your spouse, but then also make choices that enhance your own life. Trust God to help you put together the big and little details of your life.

a. What special interests can I pursue at this time?

b. How can I use my time and energy most wisely to meet my needs and enhance my marriage relationship?

8. Walk by faith. "Now faith is being sure of what we hope for and certain of what we do not see . . . And without faith it is impossible to please God, because anyone who comes to him must believe that he exists and that he rewards those who earnestly seek him" (Hebrews 11:1, 6). Besides the truths that God will bless you and walk beside you, there are no guarantees in life. No one knows for sure how long a marriage will last or if children will be part of that relationship. There are no promises for any particular job or any amount of success. Walk step by step, one day at a time.

a. How can I walk by faith?

b. In what specific areas of my life do I need to take the first step of faith?

9. Don't make individuality an art form, especially within your marriage relationship. It's fine to appreciate and celebrate the joys of individuality, but don't wave your individuality like a banner in the face of your spouse. Be open to how you and your spouse can operate as two people who appreciate each other's individuality. Don't shut off God from helping you understand how to operate as an individual within the marriage relationship.

How can I celebrate my individuality without hurting my spouse?

Divide into small groups of four to discuss the worksheets. Then divide into married participants and singles to talk about any questions or concerns that came up during the discussion.

During these discussions ask three volunteers to prepare to read the following verses: Philippians 3:7-8; John 15:10-11; and 1 Corinthians 3:10-15.

(5 minutes) After questions and concerns have been allayed, say: "Seek your identity in Christ. When your identity is in Christ, you can overcome difficulties and know that the Lord is in control of your life. 'I have been crucified with Christ and I no longer live, but Christ lives in me. The life I live in the body, I live by faith in the Son of God, who loved me and gave himself for me' (Galatians 2:20).

"When your identity is in Christ, you need not get caught in titles such as 'I'm single,' 'I'm married' or 'I'm divorced.' The danger of locating your identity in a title occurs when titles change. Married people can suddenly become single. Single people can suddenly decide to marry. When you identify with Christ, your identity and sense of worth are built on a solid foundation that won't change. This foundation can withstand all of life's attacks.

"When your identity is in Christ, seek to live your life for him realizing that Christ is the cause that counts." Ask the first volunteer to read Philippians 3:7-8.

"When your identity is in Christ, seek to live your life for him realizing that Christ is the cause that satisfies." Ask the next volunteer to read John 15:10-11.

"When your identity is in Christ, seek to live your life for him realizing that Christ is the cause that rewards eternally." Ask the last volunteer to read 1 Corinthians 3:10-15.

Encourage group members to comment on these verses in light of the study they have just completed on singleness.

CLOSING

(5 minutes) Ask each person to turn to the "Covenant of Individuality" and work alone.

Covenant of Individuality

Instructions: Complete the following statement, listing specific ideas on how you can work with God to celebrate your individuality as a part of his creation. For example, "I'll develop my unique gifts; I'll take voice lessons."

I will covenant with God to live out my individuality in the following ways:
1.
2.
3.
4.
5.

Have participants each share one of their ideas with the group. Close this study with the following prayer: "God, thank you for creating each one of us as individuals. Help us celebrate our individuality in the midst of those who love us as we are. May we dismiss all titles and identify ourselves and each other as your unique creations. In Christ's name we pray, amen."

Remind group members to complete the "Solo" activity for this study and return with their Study Guides to the next session. Encourage participants to read *Wide My World, Narrow My Bed: Living and Loving the Single Life* by Luci Swindoll (Multnomah) for additional information on the subject of singleness.

Introduce changing relationships with parents as the topic for the next study.

Solo

Instructions: Interview several people who are single: Visit with an individual who has always been single. Talk with a person who was married and is now single. Visit with someone who married later, after years of singleness. Ask each of these people the following questions:

1. What joys did you experience as a single?
2. What struggles did you experience as a single?
3. What part did Christ play in your life as a single?

The things I learned from these individuals about celebrating my singleness are:

How Do I Relate to My Parents?

*R*elating to one's parents gets trickier the longer a person lives. A parental relationship with a small child is fairly predictable in the early years. Then comes the strain of adolescence as the child pushes for independence. Finally, adulthood arrives. If a family is to develop or maintain a positive relationship, parents and children must cease their battles, become interdependent and recognize each other as friends.

As a young adult moves from childhood into financial independence and sometimes marriage, parental relationships have to change again. The change is difficult for everyone, but it can be done. Encourage the young adults in your group to realize they can play a positive part in this change. They have a choice: They can work to add a healthy dimension to this old relationship, continue the struggle or run the risk of being a child for the rest of their lives.

Part of the leadership role in this study is sharing your own story and talking about what you've learned about changing relationships with your own parents. Your insights will help group members immeasurably as they seek to understand relationships with their parents and to recognize the work that needs to be done. So think about how to present your own story as you begin this study. You will grow, and your group will thank you.

OBJECTIVES

In this study participants will:
- discuss the joys and difficulties of the parent-child relationship.
- discover what the Bible says about this relationship.
- determine how relationships with their parents can change as they move into adulthood.
- explore practical tips for a successful relationship with parents.
- continue to build a learning and caring community.

PREPARATION . . . .

- ☐ Study the material carefully and prayerfully.
- ☐ Gather newsprint, markers, masking tape, pencils, 3×5 cards, a basket and Bibles.
- ☐ Prepare three large signs: "a," "b" and "c." Tape the letters in order along one wall.

OPENING

(10 minutes) Remind group members that the focus for this study is how to relate to parents now that they're adults. Begin by sharing your story of how the relationship with your parents has changed. Talk about what it was like to grow up in your home, the things about your parents you did or didn't appreciate, deliberate ways you've had to work at this relationship and significant steps you've taken to facilitate particular changes.

After sharing your story, give participants each a 3×5 card. Have them make a plus sign in one corner before they start to write. Then give the following instructions: "On the side with the plus sign, write one way you appreciate your parents. You might mention something like, 'My parents respect my opinions about political issues and listen to what I have to say' or 'My parents allow me to make my own choices about my faith and never insist that I attend only their church.' " Allow a few moments for people to write.

Then say: "On the other side of the card, write one thing that frustrates you about your parents. You might say, 'My parents expect me to be at home when they call; they refuse to talk to my answering machine' or 'I continue to struggle with a poor self-concept that I developed after living in a home where I was told I probably wouldn't accomplish anything.' "

Ask participants not to sign their cards, but let them know you will collect the cards and read them to the group. After a few minutes, pass the basket to gather the cards. Ask a volunteer to make brief notes on a sheet of newsprint about what you read. Read all the appreciations first. Then read the frustrations. Encourage participants to correct or add to the lists. Leave lists on the wall while you continue your study.

EXPLORATION

(15 minutes) After a brief discussion of the lists, say: "All of us have reasons to appreciate our parents. They have given us a lot. But the parent-child relationship is also loaded with potential conflict, especially as we move into adulthood and the relationship changes. We need some guidelines on how to handle this changing relationship.

"What does the Bible say about changing relationships with parents? Some believe the Bible is quite specific. Others believe the Bible never addresses this issue. These individuals reason that changing relationships are primarily a product of Western civilization and rarely occurred thousands of years ago because of the culture of that time. But let's come with open minds and see for ourselves what the Bible says."

Divide into small groups of three. Have everyone turn to "The Bible Talks About Parental Relationships." Say, "Read the scripture passages and discuss what they say about your relationship with your parents."

The Bible Talks About Parental Relationships

Instructions: Read the following scripture passages and answer the questions that follow. Discuss your answers within your small group.

Specific Directions:
1. "For this reason a man will leave his father and mother and be united to his wife, and they will become one flesh" (Genesis 2:24).
a. Why are specific directions to leave one's parents necessary when a couple decides to marry?

b. What does this say about parent-child relationships?

2. ''Honor your father and your mother, so that you may live long in the land the Lord your God is giving you'' (Exodus 20:12).
a. What does it mean to ''honor your father and your mother''?

b. How does to ''live long in the land the Lord your God is giving you'' relate to the parent-child relationship? What does this phrase mean?

3. ''Children, obey your parents in the Lord, for this is right'' (Ephesians 6:1).
''Children, obey your parents in everything, for this pleases the Lord'' (Colossians 3:20).
a. Is it always right to obey your parents? Explain.

b. Does the phrase ''in the Lord'' alter this direction? Explain.

Jesus' Example:
1. Jesus never married, but he did become independent of his parents. His independence, however, didn't stop him from honoring and loving his family. Look at Jesus' example in the following scripture passages and work together to draw some conclusions about the parent-child relationship involved.
''On the third day a wedding took place at Cana in Galilee. Jesus' mother was there, and Jesus and his disciples had also been invited to the wedding. When the wine was gone, Jesus' mother said to him, 'They have no more wine.'
'' 'Dear woman, why do you involve me?' Jesus replied. 'My time has not yet come.'
''His mother said to the servants, 'Do whatever he tells you.'
''Nearby stood six stone water jars, the kind used by the Jews for ceremonial washing, each holding from twenty to thirty gallons.
''Jesus said to the servants, 'Fill the jars with water'; so they filled them to the brim.
''Then he told them, 'Now draw some out and take it to the master of the banquet.'
''They did so, and the master of the banquet tasted the water that had been turned into wine. He did not realize where it had come from, though the servants who had drawn the water knew. Then he called the bridegroom aside and said, 'Everyone brings out the choice wine first and then the cheaper wine after the guests have had too much to drink; but you have saved the best till now.'
''This, the first of his miraculous signs, Jesus performed in Cana of Galilee. He thus revealed his glory, and his disciples put their faith in him'' (John 2:1-11).
a. How would you characterize Jesus' relationship with his mother in this passage?

b. Did their relationship influence this experience? Why or why not?

c. What would you conclude from this passage?

2. ''Then Jesus entered a house, and again a crowd gathered, so that he and his disciples were not even able to eat. When his family heard about this, they went to take charge of him, for they said, 'He is out of his mind' . . . Then

Jesus' mother and brothers arrived. Standing outside, they sent someone in to call him. A crowd was sitting around him, and they told him, 'Your mother and brothers are outside looking for you.'

" 'Who are my mother and my brothers?' he asked.

"Then he looked at those seated in a circle around him and said, 'Here are my mother and my brothers! Whoever does God's will is my brother and sister and mother' " (Mark 3:20-21, 31-35).

a. What was the motive of Jesus' family in coming to see him?

b. How did their motive affect Jesus? How did he respond to their concern?

c. What would you conclude from this passage?

3. "Near the cross of Jesus stood his mother, his mother's sister, Mary the wife of Clopas, and Mary Magdalene. When Jesus saw his mother there, and the disciple whom he loved standing nearby, he said to his mother, 'Dear woman, here is your son,' and to the disciple, 'Here is your mother.' From that time on, this disciple took her into his home" (John 19:25-27).

a. What was Jesus' concern here?

b. How did he take care of this concern?

c. What would you conclude from this passage?

Your Conclusions:
Reflecting on these scripture passages and everything else you know about Jesus, write a brief statement of 20 words or less describing how Jesus views your relationship with your parents, especially as you mature into an adult.

Tape a sheet of newsprint to the wall. Have several volunteers read their statements. On the newsprint, list the different conclusions on what these passages mean. Ask participants to point out the similarities and the differences they see. Ask the group: "With which of these conclusions do you agree or disagree? Why?"

(10 minutes) After a brief discussion, say: "It's unlikely that we will totally agree on how to handle parental relationships, especially since most of us were raised by different parents in different home situations. But the question remains the same: When should a relationship with parents change from a parent-to-child relationship to an adult-to-adult relationship?"

Ask participants to stand in front of the wall on which you taped the letters "a," "b" and "c." Say: "When should your relationship with your parents change? Each time I read this question, I will give you three options from which to choose. Stand under the letter of the option that most closely represents your position. Be prepared to explain why you chose that option to the people who made the same choice you did."

Read each question with its three options. Encourage participants to make a choice, and allow time for group members to explain why they made that choice.

1. When should your relationship with your parents change?
    a. When you enter high school.
    b. When you reach age 18.
    c. When you graduate from high school.
2. When should your relationship with your parents change?
    a. When you go away to college.
    b. When you get a job.
    c. When you marry.
3. When should your relationship with your parents change?
    a. When you move out of your parents' home.
    b. When you are no longer financially supported by your parents.
    c. When your life choices no longer agree with those of your parents.
4. When should your relationship with your parents change?
    a. Never.
    b. When you decide.
    c. When your parents decide.

Have the group be seated and ask: "Which of these options seemed most appropriate for you? Why? Would you add any other suggestion to the options given?"

(15 minutes) After this opportunity to discuss each other's opinions, say: "We've had a chance to talk about *when* relationships should change. Now let's look at some practical tips on *how* to make these changes work for you and your parents. Since there is no way to make someone else change, these tips concentrate on you and how you can help make this experience as pleasant and effective as possible.

"Turn to 'How to Relate to Your Parents.' " Have different people read the suggested tips. Then ask participants to answer the questions solo.

How to Relate to Your Parents

Instructions: After listening to the suggested tips, work alone to answer the questions at the end of this worksheet.

1. Be patient with your parents. Remember, they've been adults for a long time and are probably somewhat set in their ways. They may not understand your need for adventure and risk or your desire for new and varied experiences. So be patient with them.

2. Listen to your parents. These people know you well and normally have your best interests in mind. Look beyond their words when their reasoning seems unclear to you. They may have a hunch they can't express. Their reasoning may be wrong, but their conclusions might be right.

3. Recognize yourself and your parents as unique creations of God. God created each one of you. No one else is exactly like you or either of your parents. The Bible says: "For you created my inmost being; you knit me together in my mother's womb. I praise you because I am fearfully and wonderfully made; your works are wonderful, I know that full well. My frame was not hidden from you when I was made in the secret place. When I was woven together in the depths of the earth, your eyes saw my unformed body. All the days ordained for me were written in your book before one of them came to be" (Psalm 139:13-16).

Look to God to find out why you have the parents you do. God wasn't surprised by who your parents were. He knew who they would be before you were born, probably before they were born. His design allowed you to have the parents you have. Think about what God wants these parents to teach you about life. What can you learn from them as you mature into adulthood?

4. Communicate with your parents about changes that are going on. Your parents probably will have more difficulty adjusting to your new-found autonomy and freedom than you will. For years they have played a significant role in determining the direction your life has taken. They made sure you got to baseball practice on time. They bought you that first guitar. They helped you understand your responsibilities both at home and with others. They want and need to know what's happening in your life today. Make them as much a part of your life as you can.

5. Try to put yourself in your parents' place as you work through this time of transition. Changing from a dependent child to an independent adult is bound to produce tension, both for you and your parents. When this tension occurs, strengths and weaknesses may emerge. Emotions can appear at any time in varying degrees. Try to listen to each other and understand the other person's point of view.

Use this scripture as a guideline for your relationship with your parents: "Do nothing out of selfish ambition or vain conceit, but in humility consider others better than yourselves. Each of you should look not only to your own interests, but also to the interests of others" (Philippians 2:3-4).

6. Open yourself to change. If you want your parents to change, be open to the possibility of change for yourself. The turbulent teenage and young adult years can be rough on everyone in a family. Mistrust and hurt feelings can develop. Your parents are probably hoping you'll change as much as you're hoping they will. So open yourself and be willing to take the first step.

7. Assume your own responsibilities. When you become an adult, don't expect your parents to provide for you the way they've provided in the past. Your parents aren't your servants. Nor should they be your special source of funding or an insurance policy. With your new freedoms, you've gained additional responsibilities. That's part of the maturation process.

8. Take your parents off their pedestals. Remember your parents are real people; they aren't perfect. They have needs, strengths and weaknesses. They have their positive points and their negative ones, just like you do.

As you become an adult, think of your parents as equals. Accept their mistakes. Understand their hurts. View their positive attributes more clearly.

Learn to listen to your parents' needs. They need to be trusted. They need to be loved. They need to hear that you love them. They need to know it's okay to make mistakes. They get lonely, they feel pain and they get frustrated. Don't forget, your parents are people just like you; treat them as you want them to treat you.

9. Let your parents know that you love and appreciate them by your words and actions. Surprise them by writing a thank-you note for something specific they've done. Do something practical like buying the groceries or washing their car, even if they didn't ask you to do it. Express an interest in their work, their golf game or some other part of their life. Let them experience your love and appreciation in a real and positive way.

10. Remember God's commandment to honor your father and your mother. To honor means to prize highly, to care for, to show deep respect for, to obey. As you move toward the age where you're no longer required to obey your parents, think about how you can continue to honor them. Think of specific ways you can do that.

11. Learn how to make your own decisions as an adult independent from your parents. Sometimes you will find yourself trying to win your parents' approval by doing something you think you should do, rather than thinking about what God would have you do. Unconsciously, you are still trying to win your parents' approval instead of developing the unique skills of decision-making God has given you. Concentrate on developing your personal skills instead of depending on your parents.

12. If your parents have hurt you, forgive them. This may be a painfully slow process, but it's absolutely necessary for your relationship and your peace of mind. Forgiveness is the only way you can grow up emotionally and move on to an adult relationship with your parents.

13. Keep in contact with your parents. When you get away from home, it's easy to lose touch with your parents. Call them. Write them. When you get a letter from home, read it carefully. What can you learn about them? What can you learn about yourself? Remember this relationship continues for a lifetime.

Questions to Consider:
1. Which of these points has been most helpful to you?

2. How would you like to see your relationship with your parents change?

3. What do you need to do to help make this change happen?

CLOSING

(5 minutes) Say: "Your relationship with your parents has been changing since you were born, but it has changed more drastically as you've matured into adulthood. For 18 years your parents assumed key roles in your life: providers, nurturers, disciplinarians, directors and so on. They gave you a shoulder to cry on, a pat on the back or a stern lecture, depending upon your needs.

"As you moved into adolescence, your perceptions of your parents changed even more. You realized your father wasn't really the strongest man in the world. And you found that your mother wasn't actually the smartest woman alive. These two people certainly didn't dress as well as you thought they should. Sometimes they didn't even seem to understand how the real world functioned. They certainly didn't know how to have fun, nor did they understand you and your need to have fun.

"As you've grown older, your perceptions have continued to change. As your parents loosened their controls and encouraged you to take authority in your own life, you moved into adulthood. Think about the kind of relationship you can have now with your parents.

"Take a few moments to think about what you want your relationship with your parents to be. What personal quality can you bring to that relationship to make it special?"

After a few moments, close with the following prayer: "God, you have given us our parents. You have been with our families through the easy years and also during difficult times. Help us understand and accept our parents as they are. Give all our family members the ability to use our likenesses to enjoy each other's presence. Help us use our differences to grow. Give us the strength to accept each other's changes as ways to know each other better. In the name of your Son we pray, amen."

Encourage participants to complete the "Solo" activity in their Study Guides. Suggest they read Dr. Ronald W. Richardson's book *Family Ties That Bind* (Self-Counsel). Remind them to bring their books back to the next study about relationships with brothers and sisters or how to operate as an "only."

Solo

Instructions: Reread the suggested tips in "How to Relate to Your Parents." Write two or three tips on which you want to concentrate. Decide how you would like to work on these tips and take at least one positive step this week. For example, if you have decided to keep in contact with your parents, make that phone call.

Tips on Which I Want to Concentrate	Things I Want to Do
1.	
2.	
3.	

An Opportunity for Growth:
Talk with your parents in the near future and go through these practical tips. Talk about how you and your parents can work at this new relationship. Ask your parents to come up with other guidelines to add to the list.

All in the Family: Relating With Brothers and Sisters or as an Only Child

*H*ow well do you relate to your brothers and sisters? Do you have trouble understanding how you and your siblings are different even though you came from the same home? How can you learn to relate to other family members with greater understanding and deeper love? These are some of the questions this study addresses as participants look at one of the most complicated relationships of all—getting along with the "other kids" in the family. The intent of this study is to help group members improve their relationships with siblings.

One key area of this study will center on birth order—how it influences who individuals are and how they relate as brothers and sisters. Even though the siblings' environment may be the same or similar, the fact that an individual is an eldest, a middle or a youngest child reflects unique qualities in his or her personality. Learning about birth order gives individuals greater empathy in understanding themselves and their older or younger siblings. In addition, examining the unique situation of only children will help them and others better understand their special struggles. Empathy and understanding are important steps to improving family relationships.

Encourage group members to open their eyes, ears and hearts for a clearer understanding of these important relationships.

OBJECTIVES

In this study participants will:

● look at birth order and the general characteristics for first-born, middle-born, last-born and only children.

● relate these characteristics to their own birth order and placement of siblings in their families.

● process this information to help them understand themselves and their siblings better.

● use this information to improve relationships among family members.

● continue to grow as part of a caring, sharing and loving community of learners.

PREPARATION . . . .

☐ Study the material carefully and prayerfully.

☐ Purchase a box of crayons for each group of four people or use an assortment of broken crayons for all groups.

☐ Gather pencils and Bibles.

☐ Prepare a "When Can We Eat?" worksheet ahead of time for participants to see as an example.

OPENING

(10 minutes) Say: "As we continue our study on relationships, let's examine the family even further. Last week, we talked about relating to our parents. In this study we're going to talk about relating to brothers and sisters. And if you happen to be an only child, we're going to talk about what that means for you as well." Divide participants into groups of four. Distribute crayons to each group. Then give the following instructions: "Turn to 'When Can We Eat?' This fun exercise will provide us with some good insights into our home life. Think back to mealtime at your house when you were growing up. Draw a picture of the family table in the space provided

and indicate as accurately as possible where everyone in your family sat around that table. Use symbols and colors to represent each member of your family. For instance, your dad may have sat at the head of the table. In your mind, he was the rock of your home, even though there didn't seem to be much color or joy in his life. He was a solid citizen, and you felt comforted and secure knowing he was so reliable. At the head of the table, draw a gray rock with smooth edges to represent your dad. Continue until you've drawn a symbol and used a color for each member of your family around the table." Present the family table worksheet you've prepared ahead of time as an example.

When Can We Eat?

Instructions: Draw a table to represent the family table you used when you were growing up. Choose a color and a symbol to represent each member of your family. Draw each symbol in a location that indicates where that person sat at the table.

When individuals have completed their drawings, have people explain them to their small group. After all drawings are explained, regroup and ask, "What insights did you gain from these drawings?"

EXPLORATION

(10 minutes) Say: "From your comments (and my own experiences), I know it's not easy to get along with siblings. Some siblings fight with each other, while others run away or just avoid their brothers and sisters. Sibling relationships have been difficult since the beginning of time. Those of you who are only children may not have experienced these particular conflicts, but you may begin to realize why other family struggles have occurred as you listen to others. Let's examine a couple of biblical examples of sibling rivalry."

Have someone read the story of Cain and Abel in Genesis 4:3-9. When he or she is finished, ask: "Why did Cain kill his brother? What do we learn about sibling relationships in these verses?"

Assign several people to read Genesis 37:1-36. You will need different readers for the different parts, including a narrator; the father, Israel; Joseph; the brothers, including Reuben and Judah; and the man in the field. After the group reads the story together, ask: "Why was there conflict between these brothers? How did the conflict affect the relationships? What do we learn about sibling relationships from this story?"

(5 minutes) After a brief discussion, say: "From these passages, we learned that sibling rivalry has existed for centuries. Jealousy or parental favoritism can trigger these negative conflicts, but God designed people to live together in harmony, even in the family. 'How good and pleasant it is when brothers live together in unity' (Psalm 133:1).

"One way we can help this relationship is to better understand ourselves, our siblings and the dynamics of our families. It also helps to understand the concept of birth order. Recent studies have offered important insights on what it means to be a firstborn, middle-born, last-born or an only child and how that position affects us and our view of the world.

"Today, we're going to look at some of that research, ask some questions and gain some understanding of the influence of family positioning. As we examine these characteristics, realize these observations are generalizations. It's also significant to note that there is more information about firstborns because every family, including those with just one child, has a firstborn. Also, many firstborn males in some cultures fall under the 'firstborn' category, even though they may not be the oldest in their families. With the addition of each new child into a family, the environment changes and family dynamics shift. This situation helps explain that even though you were raised by the same parents and grew up in the same house, the environment is different with each child. Let's look at these characteristics."

(20 minutes) Ask participants to form four groups based on their position in the family—a firstborn group, middle-born group, last-born group and only-child group. If individuals are unsure of where they belong because of death or blended families, tell them to choose the position they would use to describe themselves to their best friends. Have group members turn to "Birth Order: How to Understand and Use It Effectively." Tell the group the birth order descriptions have been adapted from *The Birth Order Book* by Dr. Kevin Leman (Revell). Ask each group to read and discuss the birth order suggestions and follow the directions on the worksheet.

Birth Order: How to Understand and Use It Effectively ▬

Instructions: Read and discuss the birth order suggestions that apply to you. Discuss the first set of questions in your small group. Then read the suggestions for the *other* birth order positions. If you have siblings, discuss the questions about siblings. If you are an only child, discuss the questions directed at you.

Firstborns

Description: conscientious, perfectionist, reliable. People look up to you, trust you and feel they can count on you. But beware of how your strengths can become weaknesses. Here are some suggestions:

1. Take smaller bites of life. Firstborns are known for getting themselves too involved in too many things. They wind up with little time for themselves.

2. Work on saying no. Firstborns are pleasers; they like the approval of others and almost always accept invitations, requests, etc. Recognize your limits and say no. Remember, you can't do everything.

3. As a firstborn, your parents probably had higher expectations for you than anybody else in the family; therefore, you naturally have high expectations for yourself. You expect perfection, which is a great way to commit slow suicide. Lower your sights a little. Do less and enjoy life more.

4. Firstborns are known for asking lots of questions and wanting all details. Don't apologize for this trait. A leader can size up a situation, outline what has to be done and apply a logical, step-by-step process to solve the problem.

5. As a firstborn you may be cautious and careful. Don't let people pressure you into jumping into things when you need time to make your decision.

6. If you are the serious type, try to develop a sense of humor. Learn to laugh at your mistakes. You're bound to fail now and then. Mistakes are a great way to learn and improve.

7. Never apologize for being conscientious and overorganized. As a first-born you need structure; you need your "to do" lists. But don't be driven by all this. Enjoy being organized and well-planned, and share your skills with others. A lot of people around you could use this kind of help!

Your Personal Birth Order Suggestions:

1. How appropriate was your birth order description?

2. Which suggestions fit? Which ones didn't? Why or why not?

3. Which suggestions indicate a need for personal change? Explain.

Your Sibling's Birth Order Suggestions:

1. Is the description accurate for your sibling? Why or why not?

2. Which suggestions for your sibling did you not understand until now? Explain.

3. In what areas do you see a need for understanding on your part? How will improving these areas of understanding improve your relationship with your sibling?

Middle Borns

Description: sometimes come off as people to be pitied, receive hand-me-downs, have fewer photos in the family album and feel like outsiders or fifth wheels. While firstborns and last borns may get more attention, middle children get better training for life. If you are a middle child, instead of feeling deprived, make the most of the tools you have gained while growing up. Here are some suggestions:

1. You probably have people-oriented social skills because of all the negotiating and mediating you had to do while growing up. Use these skills to see both sides and deal with life as it really is.

2. "I'm really not much of a negotiator—I'm more of a free spirit. I like to do my thing." If anybody is unpredictable, it's a middle child. If you are the free-spirit type, fight to keep your unique qualities. Businesses and companies are often looking for someone with new ideas and the independence to try them.

3. Middle children often grow up telling themselves, "No one listens to me, not even my family." Instead of apologizing for your opinions, or failing to offer them at all, discuss your ideas with others. Many people are looking for someone who's willing to offer his or her input but not do all the talking.

4. If the "socially skilled, lots of friends" label fits you, enjoy it. But don't spread yourself too thin. No one can maintain a limitless number of relationships and keep them meaningful.

5. Don't get sucked into comparisons. There will always be people who are above or below you in terms of ability, interest, appearance, athletic skill, etc. Comparisons are futile and usually pointless. Just be comfortable being yourself.

6. Don't think firstborns are the only people who can lead others. Middle children often make excellent managers and leaders because they understand compromise and negotiation. If you are in a position to try for a manager's slot, don't hesitate because you think you don't have the charisma or dynamics to succeed. Use your natural middle-child skills to go for it!

Your Personal Birth Order Suggestions:
1. How appropriate was your birth order description?
2. Which suggestions fit? Which ones didn't? Why or why not?
3. Which suggestions indicate a need for personal change? Explain.

Your Sibling's Birth Order Suggestions:
1. Is the description accurate for your sibling? Why or why not?
2. Which suggestions for your sibling did you not understand until now? Explain.
3. In what areas do you see a need for understanding on your part? How will improving these areas of understanding improve your relationships with your sibling?

Last Borns

Description: like to be taken care of, enjoy relationships with others, think a lot about "how things will benefit me." If you are the baby of your family, some of the following suggestions can help you cope with life as an employee, spouse, parent and friend.

1. Accept responsibility for yourself and your actions. Stop "passing the buck." You're not a little kid anymore, so why continue to act like one?

2. Many last borns are "messies." Pick up after yourself. Your spouse will call you blessed and your mother may say, "I never thought I'd see the day."

3. You are likely a people person and will find the most opportunity and satisfaction in working with people. Consider changing jobs, even if it means a temporary cut in pay. Any job that requires interaction with people like sales is a strong possibility. Consider a managerial position, only as long as you feel you can keep things organized and on schedule.

4. Although last borns are usually people persons, ironically they struggle with self-centeredness. When you offer help to others, follow through and do it quietly without fanfare. Help others by sharing your money, time and energy; sharing is a great cure for self-centeredness.

5. Beware of being too independent. Admit your faults. Don't blame others when you know you're responsible.

6. Recognize your gift to be funny, charming and persuasive—assets in any situation. Beware, however, of always working for that pat on the head and asking, "What's in it for me?"

7. If you love attention, be advised that others also like it now and then. When talking with others, always ask them about their plans, their feelings and what they think.

8. Before marriage, try dating firstborns. You may find these individuals most compatible. After marriage to any birth order, remember that your wife is not your mother, your husband is not your father.

Your Personal Birth Order Suggestions:
1. How appropriate was your birth order description?
2. Which suggestions fit? Which ones didn't? Why or why not?
3. Which suggestions indicate a need for personal change? Explain.

Your Sibling's Birth Order Suggestions:
1. Is the description accurate for your sibling? Why or why not?
2. Which suggestions for your sibling did you not understand until now? Explain.
3. In what areas do you see a need for understanding on your part? How will improving these areas of understanding improve your relationship with your sibling?

Only Children

Description: superconscientious, reliable, "firstborns in duplicate." All of the tips for firstborns are also applicable here. (Read those suggestions at this point.) If you are an only child, pay close attention to several other points:

1. Beware of making too many commitments or expecting too much of yourself. You can get caught in a daily "rat race," with no end in sight.

2. Build time and space for yourself into a busy schedule. Only children need time for themselves; make sure it happens.

3. Only children tend to get along better with people much older or much younger than themselves. Try to arrange for experiences with older and younger people who will give you more strokes and argue with you less.

4. Only children are often labeled selfish and self-centered because they've never learned how to share with others. Take an honest inventory of your own life. Think about how you act around your spouse, friends or fellow workers. What specific things can you do to put others first, help others more and be less critical of others?

Your Personal Birth Order Suggestions:
1. How appropriate was your birth order description?
2. Which suggestions fit? Which ones didn't? Why or why not?
3. Which suggestions indicate a need for personal change? Explain.

Discussion Questions for Only Children:
After reading the other descriptions, answer the following questions.
1. Do any of the other descriptions fit you more accurately? Why or why not?
2. Which descriptions and suggestions for others surprised you? Why?
3. How can your understanding of these suggestions help you improve relationships with your parents? your friends? your co-workers?

CLOSING

(10 minutes) Call the groups back together. Ask participants to share one thing they have learned about themselves and how that

knowledge will improve relationships among siblings or others in the family. Then ask participants to share one thing they've learned about their siblings or siblings in general that will help them establish a better family relationship.

Close with the following statement: "I hope you've been encouraged by a better understanding of yourself and your siblings. I encourage you to commit yourself to appreciating differences among you and your siblings. Work on being patient and understanding with others. Talk with one another about the differences you see. Affirm your siblings or closest family members for their unique qualities."

Quote the following scripture passage: "Then Peter came to Jesus and asked, 'Lord, how many times shall I forgive my brother when he sins against me? Up to seven times?'

"Jesus answered, 'I tell you, not seven times, but seventy-seven times' " (Matthew 18:21-22). Say: "No matter how much you understand your brothers and sisters, there will be past and future offenses that need forgiveness. Take the understandings you have gained from this study and use them to affirm and forgive siblings and other family members."

Conclude with the following prayer: "God, we recognize our positions in our families. We have examined what it means to be a firstborn, middle-born, last-born or an only child. Help us understand what we read and use that understanding to create a deeper relationship with our siblings and those closest to us. Use us as instruments of peace and understanding within family conflicts. Help us experience your gift of grace in those relationships that are essential for a healthy family life. In your Son's name we pray, amen."

Explain the "Solo" activity in the Study Guide, and remind participants to bring their books back for the next study about relationships in the work place. Encourage individuals who want to pursue this subject further to read *The Birth Order Book* by Dr. Kevin Leman (Revell).

Instructions: Call, write or visit with one of your siblings and/or parents to talk about birth order. Read "Birth Order: How to Understand and Use It Effectively" and discuss any insights you might have had. Use the discussion questions to stimulate conversation, and decide on ways to make family relationships healthier.

1. List ways to improve relationships with your siblings or parents.

2. Choose one idea and decide how both of you will implement this idea in your relationship.

3. Pray for each other—for your relationship,
for your failures,
for your successes,
for God's presence in your efforts.

Relationships in the Work Place

*T*oo many people compartmentalize their lives. They separate their work from their faith. Business is business, and church is church. God never intended the two to be separate. How people work represents a part of who they are, which includes their relationship with their Creator.

This study gets back to the basic concepts for work. God intends for his people to work, and God wants them to represent him in their work place. (Going to school and managing a home count as work!) Encourage your young adults to concentrate on building relationships on the job.

OBJECTIVES

In this study participants will:

- gain a biblical perspective on work.
- become a positive force in their work place by seeing them-

selves as Christ's representatives.

    ● discuss how they can be more effective in the employee-to-employer relationship, the employer-to-employee relationship and the employee-to-employee relationship.

    ● continue to build a loving and supportive community of learners.

PREPARATION ....

    ☐ Study the material carefully and prayerfully.
    ☐ Gather newsprint, markers, masking tape, pencils, paper cups and Bibles.

OPENING

(10 minutes) Welcome the group and introduce this study by saying: "This week we're going to look at a four-letter word that's troubled a lot of people—W-O-R-K. We're going to examine that word from a biblical perspective and then seek to understand what God wants for us in three different work-related relationships: employee to employer, employer to employee and employee to employee."

Give participants each a paper cup. Ask them to mold the cup so it illustrates the type of representative for Christ they've been on the job, or at school if they are not yet working. Let them know they can alter the cup in any way; they can rip it, change its shape or do whatever they want. One person might make the cup into a box and say: "I've boxed in my faith. By compartmentalizing my life, I've drawn a distinction between my work and my faith. I've never made a conscious effort to be Christ's representative on my job." Another person might leave the cup as it is and say: "I've tried to give a cup of cold water in Jesus' name to those who have been thirsty at work. I haven't always succeeded, but I think I've done fairly well." After all participants have molded their cups, explain your cup to the group. Then have the rest of the group explain what they've done to their cups and what it means to them.

EXPLORATION

(20 minutes) After everyone has had a chance to share, say: "When God created people, he also gave them a task. Let's listen to several passages in Genesis that explain God's plan." Ask someone in advance to read Genesis 1:28 and 2:15. Explain: "God gave human

beings a vocational assignment at the beginning. When perfect harmony and an ideal relationship existed between God and his creations, work was a vital part of God's design. Work got tougher only after the Fall of humanity."

Ask a volunteer to read Genesis 3:17-19. Then say: "But work was still part of what God wanted his creations to do. Some can be temporarily unemployed either because of poor performance or through no fault of their own, but God calls no one to permanent unemployment. God wants everyone to work; no one is exempt. Since this course is devoted to relationships and since each of us will spend much of our life working, let's focus on the concept of how we can use our jobs and professions as ambassadors for Christ."

Have participants turn to "Christ's Ambassadors at Work." Introduce this worksheet by asking, "What is an ambassador?" Most people will have some idea or be able to name a few. Try to get to the following definitions: "a special representative" or "an official agent with a special mission." Then say: "God calls us to full-time Christian service. He has put individuals in particular situations with tasks he wants us to accomplish. Our tasks may include developing a relationship with an impossible personality, witnessing in the midst of a tough situation or learning some particular lesson to prepare us for life. When we leave a job prematurely, surrender or quit before we allow the Lord to use this experience, we fail as ambassadors for Christ.

"Give your job to the Lord. Play the role of ambassador. Besides improving your work performance, God can use you in powerful ways." Ask participants to complete this worksheet alone.

Christs's Ambassadors at Work ▬▬▬▬▬▬

Instructions: Follow directions for each part of this worksheet.

Paul's Thoughts on Work:

Read what Paul had to say about work. Summarize Paul's teachings at the end of this section. Be specific.

"We work hard with our own hands" (1 Corinthians 4:12a).

"Make it your ambition to lead a quiet life, to mind your own business and to work with your hands, just as we told you, so that your daily life may win the respect of outsiders and so that you will not be dependent on anybody" (1 Thessalonians 4:11-12).

"Now we ask you, brothers, to respect those who work hard among you, who are over you in the Lord and who admonish you. Hold them in the highest regard in love because of their work" (1 Thessalonians 5:12-13a).

"For even when we were with you, we gave you this rule: 'If a man will not work, he shall not eat'" (2 Thessalonians 3:10).

Summarize Paul's teachings:

Portrait of an Ambassador:

Read the following scripture passages and comment on how each passage applies to work.

1. Think about what you were.

"As for you, you were dead in your transgressions and sins . . . Remember that at that time you were separate from Christ, excluded from citizenship in Israel and foreigners to the covenants of the promise, without hope and without God in the world" (Ephesians 2:1, 12).

How do these verses apply to work?

2. Think about what you are.

"Then you will know the truth, and the truth will set you free" (John 8:32).

"For God did not give us a spirit of timidity, but a spirit of power, of love and of self-discipline" (2 Timothy 1:7).

"In the same way, let your light shine before men, that they may see your good deeds and praise your Father in heaven" (Matthew 5:16).

"If anyone speaks, he should do it as one speaking the very words of God. If anyone serves, he should do it with the strength God provides, so that in all things God may be praised through Jesus Christ" (1 Peter 4:11a).

"This is to my Father's glory, that you bear much fruit, showing yourselves to be my disciples" (John 15:8).

"He will bring glory to me by taking from what is mine and making it known to you" (John 16:14).

How do these verses apply to work?

3. Think about what you do.

"Do not think that I have come to abolish the Law or the Prophets; I have not come to abolish them but to fulfill them. I tell you the truth, until heaven and earth disappear, not the smallest letter, not the least stroke of a pen, will by any means disappear from the Law until everything is accomplished. Anyone who breaks one of the least of these commandments and teaches others to do the same will be called least in the kingdom of heaven, but whoever practices and teaches these commands will be called great in the kingdom of heaven. For I tell you that unless your righteousness surpasses that of the Pharisees and the teachers of the law, you will certainly not enter the kingdom of heaven" (Matthew 5:17-20).

"Do everything without complaining or arguing, so that you may become blameless and pure, children of God without fault in a crooked and depraved generation, in which you shine like stars in the universe" (Philippians 2:14-15).

"Then Jesus came to them and said, 'All authority in heaven and on earth has been given to me. Therefore go and make disciples of all nations, baptizing them in the name of the Father and of the Son and of the Holy Spirit, and teaching them to obey everything I have commanded you. And surely I am with you always, to the very end of the age' " (Matthew 28:18-20).

How do these verses apply to work?

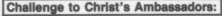

Challenge to Christ's Ambassadors:

Read the following scripture passages and answer the questions that follow. "Therefore, if anyone is in Christ, he is a new creation; the old has gone, the new has come! All this is from God, who reconciled us to himself through Christ and gave us the ministry of reconciliation: that God was reconciling the world to himself in Christ, not counting men's sins against them. And he has committed to us the message of reconciliation. We are therefore Christ's ambassadors, as though God were making his appeal through us. We implore you on Christ's behalf: Be reconciled to God. God made him who had no sin to be sin for us, so that in him we might become the righteousness of God" (2 Corinthians 5:17-21).

1. What specifically has Christ done for you?

"And pray in the Spirit on all occasions with all kinds of prayers and requests. With this in mind, be alert and always keep on praying for all the saints. Pray also for me, that whenever I open my mouth, words may be given me so that I will fearlessly make known the mystery of the gospel, for which I am an ambassador in chains. Pray that I may declare it fearlessly, as I should" (Ephesians 6:18-20).

2. What insights about being an ambassador did you receive from this passage?

3. How do Christ's actions affect your being his ambassador at *work*?

Remind participants: "You are an ambassador no matter where you are. Christ wants you to represent him at work too. Think about the following principles for the work place.

"Establish your priorities. You are first a Christian. Put God first, and he will help you become a more productive employee or employer.

"Allow the Holy Spirit to do the convicting. You don't have to be the conscience for everyone in your work place.

"Pray for the people with whom you work, the Christians as well as the non-Christians. Even if you can't stand a certain person, ask God to help you love him or her.

"Talk naturally about your relationship with God. Those around you talk freely about their interests and activities. You should feel free to do the same."

Conclude this discussion by asking the group, "How would you summarize the concept of being Christ's ambassador at work?" Write group members' responses on newsprint and work with participants to prepare a few sentences that present an accurate statement of the ideas presented. Tape this statement to the wall and leave it there throughout the rest of the study.

(10 minutes) Introduce the next activity by saying, "We want to

continue our study of relationships in the work place by looking specifically at the three relationships involved: the employee-to-employer relationship, the employer-to-employee relationship and the employee-to-employee relationship." Ask the following discussion questions:

1. How many of you have ever been employers or supervisors?

2. Did that position change the way you related to others on the job when you were the employee or under supervision? Explain your answer.

3. How many of you have had a struggle with a boss at one time or another? (Ask for examples.) How did this struggle affect your work?

4. How many of you have ever had difficulty with a co-worker? (Ask for examples.) How did this difficulty affect your work?

Try to get people to think about the difficulties and complexities of relationships in the work place. Ask group members to break into small groups of four people. Say: "When you get in your small group, discuss the 'Work Profile Questions' in your Study Guide. Move on to 'Principles of Working Relationships' after everyone has had a chance to share."

Work Profile Questions

Instructions: Discuss the following questions in your small group. After everyone has had a chance to share, turn to "Principles of Working Relationships" and continue your discussion.

1. What was the best job you've ever had? Why was it so good?

2. What kind of job do you have now? (Going to school and managing a home count as jobs!) Describe the best and the worst parts about this job.

3. What kind of job would you like to have in the future? Why? What would be the good and the bad parts about this job you want?

(10 minutes) After five minutes say, "If you haven't finished discussing the 'Work Profile Questions,' finish those quickly and move on to 'Principles of Working Relationships.'"

Principles of Working Relationships ▬▬▬▬▬

Instructions: Read the principles for all three relationships and discuss suggested questions.

● Circle those principles you think are most important. Give examples in which these principles have proved accurate.

● Put question marks beside those principles you feel are questionable.

● At the end of each section, add other principles that should be included.

Employee to Employer:

1. If you say you're going to do something, do it. Employers look for dependability and consistency. When you accept a job, make it your pride and joy. Give it your full effort, but be realistic. Two things that frustrate an employer are missed deadlines and surprising problems, so communicate with your employer throughout any task.

2. Write things out. Let your employer know what's going on. Your communication doesn't have to be fancy; most employers prefer crisp, concise memos. Written communication lets your employer know you are thinking about him or her and are concerned about the project.

3. Know your job. Listen to your boss about his or her expectations. Repeat instructions so he or she knows there is no misunderstanding. Then do the best job you can.

4. Envision God as your boss. Ask yourself: If God were my boss, would it change my work habits or my performance? "And whatever you do, whether in word or deed, do it all in the name of the Lord Jesus, giving thanks to God the Father through him . . . Whatever you do, work at it with all your heart, as working for the Lord, not for men" (Colossians 3:17, 23).

What does this passage say about the employee-to-employer relationship?

5. Don't overemphasize money. Many people in the work place fret, complain or give a lackluster performance because they feel they're worth more than what they're being paid. Rather than let a salary take care of itself and concentrate on doing a good job, these dissatisfied individuals concentrate on what they're *not* getting, to the detriment of their jobs.

God knows and has promised to meet your needs, not necessarily your wants. Someday you may have to request a raise, that's fine. But generally a person who concentrates on money instead of his or her job performs poorly. You know what your salary is, so concentrate on your work. "Therefore I tell you, do not worry about your life, what you will eat or drink; or about your body, what you will wear. Is not life more important than food, and the body more important than clothes? Look at the birds of the air; they do not sow or reap or store away in barns, and yet your heavenly Father feeds them. Are you not much more valuable than they? Who of you by worrying can add a single hour to his life?

"And why do you worry about clothes? See how the lilies of the field grow. They do not labor or spin. Yet I tell you that not even Solomon in all his splendor was dressed like one of these. If that is how God clothes the grass of the field, which is here today and tomorrow is thrown into the fire, will he not much more clothe you, O you of little faith? So do not worry, saying, 'What shall we eat?' or 'What shall we drink?' or 'What shall we wear?' For the pagans run after all these things, and your heavenly Father knows that you need them. But seek first his kingdom and his righteousness, and all these things will be given to you as well. Therefore do not worry about tomorrow, for tomorrow will worry about itself. Each day has enough trouble of its own'' (Matthew 6:25-34).

"For we brought nothing into the world, and we can take nothing out of it. But if we have food and clothing, we will be content with that. People who want to get rich fall into temptation and a trap and into many foolish and harmful desires that plunge men into ruin and destruction. For the love of money is a root of all kinds of evil. Some people, eager for money, have wandered from the faith and pierced themselves with many griefs" (1 Timothy 6:7-10).

What is God's perspective on money?

6. Work heartily. In the midst of missionary work, proclaiming the gospel and facing opposition, Paul worked hard at not being a burden to anyone. "For you yourselves know how you ought to follow our example. We were not idle when we were with you, nor did we eat anyone's food without paying for it. On the contrary, we worked night and day, laboring and toiling so that we would not be a burden to any of you. We did this, not because we do not have the right to such help, but in order to make ourselves a model for you to follow. For even when we were with you, we gave you this rule: 'If a man will not work, he shall not eat.'

"We hear that some among you are idle. They are not busy; they are busy-bodies. Such people we command and urge in the Lord Jesus Christ to settle down and earn the bread they eat. And as for you, brothers, never tire of doing what is right" (2 Thessalonians 3:7-13).

How does this scripture relate to the employee-to-employer relationship?

7. Maintain honesty within your relationship. "Simply let your 'Yes' be 'Yes,' and your 'No,' 'No' " (Matthew 5:37a). Eager employees who are unable to follow through with their plans damage their relationship with their employers by not recognizing their limitations. Have integrity about what you say. Don't be dishonest or untruthful. Establish a reputation for speaking the truth.

8. Don't compromise your morals. If your job puts you in a situation where you feel you must lie, manipulate or be dishonest, be true to yourself and your relationship with God. No job is worth changing your moral system. You have to live with yourself. If you commit an act that conflicts with your moral principles, you can't blame someone else. You made the choice.

9. Can you think of any other principles for the employee-to-employer relationship?

Employer to Employee:

1. Be fair and generous. Your employees will produce better if you are firm but fair. Reward employees financially and emotionally. Compliment them when they do well.

2. Don't rebuke an employee in front of other employees. Nothing destroys a relationship more quickly than public criticism. A good rule to follow is, "Praise in public; admonish in private."

3. Give employees some flexibility in their work. Allow them freedom to choose how they will do their jobs, and let them know you're available for guidance. When you delegate responsibility, make sure employees understand specifically what they are to do. Remember to give employees adequate authority so they can get their jobs done.

With responsibility and authority comes accountability. Let employees know how you will evaluate their work. Responsibility, authority and accountability are the three keys to successful delegation.

4. Encourage employees to write their own goals. Ask them to share them with you, then do everything you can to help your employees succeed. Praise people immediately when they do something right. Give them honest feedback as soon as they make a mistake, but remind them of your confidence in their abilities.

5. Can you think of any other principles for the employer-to-employee relationship?

Employee to Employee:

1. Do your own job, and don't worry about the job everyone else is doing. Avoid gossip, and don't tear others down so you'll move ahead. Encourage fellow workers. Let them know you want the best for them.

2. Listen to the people with whom you work. The work place is a great place to meet spiritual needs. As individuals reveal themselves, be alert to how God can use you. Remember, God has a purpose for you being there.

3. Put others first. When your actions contrast with the prevailing attitude of putting yourself first, others will notice. People may question your actions, so be ready with your response. "But in your hearts set apart Christ as Lord. Always be prepared to give an answer to everyone who asks you to give the reason for the hope that you have. But do this with gentleness and respect" (1 Peter 3:15).

a. How does this verse apply to you?

b. What opportunities have you had to share the good news in a work situation?

4. Don't be surprised or angry when you're treated rudely or unfairly at times. Don't retaliate. Continue to serve Christ and those around you.

5. Can you think of any other principles for the employee-to-employee relationship?

Ask group members to stay in their small groups and comment on the principles they thought were particularly relevant and the additional principles they have written. Write additional principles on newsprint so others may add these to their Study Guides.

CLOSING

(5 minutes) Remind participants, "God often uses our work to teach us something; he can use us in ways we never expected." Read "One Ambassador's Story" as a good example of the difference it can make to look at one's job through God's eyes.

One Ambassador's Story ▬▬▬▬▬▬▬▬

Six months into my job at a major accounting firm, I was miserable. I wanted out. Office gossip claimed that four or five people would soon be let go, and I felt my dismissal was quickly approaching. I wanted to quit before they fired me. I hated the work! In addition to being boring, monotonous and repetitive, it was extremely difficult and demanding. I also felt I was beginning to compromise my standards, and I knew I wasn't being a good witness for Christ on the job.

In the midst of this personal struggle, God became very real to me. I suddenly realized God wanted me to look to him each day and perform my tasks solely for him. If I were to be dismissed, then I would be fired while focusing on him. There would be no more complaining, no more compromise and no more exchanging my morals and beliefs in pursuit of money or promotions. I would utilize every opportunity I had to glorify God.

The first Monday after I had experienced this revelation from God, I prayed for strength and wisdom. I also prayed that I might encourage others and that I might rise above my situation even if I did lose my job. I decided that if my employers fired me, I wanted to know I had given my best and not merely accepted the inevitable. The next Friday, I thanked the Lord for a week of answered prayer. I thanked him for my job. I thanked him for the non-Christians with whom I worked. And I thanked him for giving me at least one more week to be his ambassador again.

This weekly process went on for several months. Instead of my employers firing me, others were let go. My work began to improve. Others in the firm requested me to work directly with them. Co-workers began to respect and express admiration for my morals and value system. Soon, different individuals wanted to hear my witness for God because they had seen it in action for months.

This whole process freed me to enjoy my job and share my relationship with God with people I never dreamed I would ever get to know. I'm glad I didn't give up. I'm glad God chose to teach me a lesson I'll never forget: Each of us can be an ambassador for Christ no matter where we are or what task we are doing.

Conclude this session by saying: "To wrap up this study in your small group, go around the circle and honestly tell the others one specific way you would like them to pray for you in your job situation. Then spend some time praying together as a group."

When group members have finished, remind them to complete the "Solo" activity during the week and bring their Study Guides back to the next session. Encourage those who are interested in pursuing this subject to read *What Color Is Your Parachute?* by Richard N. Bolles (Ten Speed). Let participants know the next two studies will deal with their relationship with God and how to keep it fresh.

Solo

Instructions: Look at the following chart and think about your typical workday.

In the first column, instead of writing what you do, list those people with whom you come in contact. For example, if you see Jane during your lunch hour, write Jane's name next to 12:30.

In the middle column, write a short description of your relationship with each person. You might describe your relationship with Jane as "pleasant but shallow."

Circle three relationships you want or need to work on.

In the last column, write the names of the relationships on which you want to work, and list specific ideas on how you can improve those relationships.

My Typical Workday			
	People with whom I come in contact	Description of relationship	What can I do to improve relationship?
7:00			
7:30			
8:00			1. _____
8:30			
9:00			
9:30			
10:00			
10:30			
11:00			
11:30			2. _____
Noon			
12:30			
1:00			
1:30			
2:00			
2:30			
3:00			3. _____
3:30			
4:00			
4:30			
5:00			
5:30			
6:00			
6:30			
7:00			

Set aside five minutes in your workday to pray for each of these relationships. After one week, ask yourself these questions:

1. Do I notice any differences in any of these relationships?

2. Am I continuing to work on and pray for these relationships?

3. Am I recognizing God's presence within these relationships?

Pray for God's help in continuing to work on these relationships. Ask yourself these same questions each month. Evaluate your progress one year later and continue to pray.

That Unique Relationship With Christ

"Who do you say that I am?" Jesus asked his disciples. That same question confronts people today as they focus on the most important relationship of all—their relationship with Christ.

In Study 8, participants talked about their life stories in relation to their parents. In this study, participants will think about their life stories again, only this time in relation to Christ. Some may be reluctant to talk about this part of their lives, but you can encourage them to be courageous by your openness and willingness to tell your own story.

When you talk about your own faith story, it will give the group a better understanding of you and how God has worked in your life, and it will help participants feel free to talk about their own stories. Your story will serve as a model.

Encourage all participants to use this study as a "hinge point"—a time when their lives can move in another direction and change dramatically as they respond to God's call.

OBJECTIVES

In this study participants will:
- discover what it means to have a personal relationship with Christ.
- talk about how that process begins and continues.
- have an opportunity to develop that relationship.
- continue building a learning, sharing and supportive community.

PREPARATION . . . .

☐ Study the material carefully and prayerfully.
☐ Gather newsprint, markers, pencils, Bibles, a basket and enough gloves or mittens for each person to have one.

OPENING

(5 minutes) Welcome group members and say: "During the past few weeks we've spent some time discussing how we need to be our own best friend before we can be a friend to others. We've talked about why we need each other. We've discovered ways we can make our friendships more meaningful. We've discussed dating, marriage and life as a single. We've looked at how we can relate to our parents and siblings as relationships change. We've also talked about relationships in the work place. For the next two weeks we're going to examine the most important relationship, the one that makes all others work.

"Think about the heroes you had when you were growing up. Who was your favorite hero? Why? Discuss your answers with two to three other people sitting near you."

EXPLORATION

(10 minutes) After each person has talked about his or her heroes, say: "We've talked about some special people in our lives. We've also examined some important relationships and talked about both the joys and struggles within these relationships. Some of you have mentioned your relationship with Christ even while you discussed other relationships. Details are different, but most of you have shared something about how your relationship with Christ has made a difference in your life. While you are still in your small group, turn to 'A Picture of Jesus Christ.' Complete the activity and discuss the questions."

A Picture of Jesus Christ

Instructions: How is Jesus Christ usually portrayed by others? Use the following symbols to identify the type of descriptions below:
TV—as Jesus is portrayed on television or in movies
H—as Jesus is portrayed in history books
A—as Jesus is viewed by the average person on the street

☐ greatest man who ever lived
☐ nice guy, helped people
☐ teacher of radical lifestyle
☐ Son of God, sacrifice for sin
☐ founder of a Western religion
☐ healer of lame and blind people
☐ a myth—made up by disciples
☐ his birth and death = two holidays
☐ inspiration for art and music
☐ curse words in certain crowds

1. Which description best portrays Jesus Christ for you?

2. Explain how this description plays a part in your life.

(5 minutes) Tell the group: "There are people who don't understand what it means to have a personal relationship with Christ. Some are confused. Some claim they don't believe at all, while others say they don't care. What we want to do today is discuss why having a relationship with Christ makes sense. What are some of the advantages of having a relationship with Christ? Give an example of how this relationship affects the rest of your life." List advantages on newsprint as participants relate their examples.

(10 minutes) Then say: "This list is impressive, but to effectively understand how this relationship begins and how it works and to better communicate these facts to others, we need to get a biblical understanding of this relationship. Let's examine what the Bible says about this most important relationship. Stay in your small group and turn to 'What Does the Bible Say?' "

What Does the Bible Say?

Instructions: Read the following scripture passages and answer the questions that follow.

Jesus' Words:
"Jesus answered, 'I am the way and the truth and the life. No one comes

to the Father except through me. If you really knew me, you would know my Father as well. From now on, you do know him and have seen him' " (John 14:6-7).

1. What does Jesus mean about knowing God and knowing him?

"Jesus replied, 'If anyone loves me, he will obey my teaching. My Father will love him, and we will come to him and make our home with him. He who does not love me will not obey my teaching. These words you hear are not my own; they belong to the Father who sent me.

" 'All this I have spoken while still with you. But the Counselor, the Holy Spirit, whom the Father will send in my name, will teach you all things and will remind you of everything I have said to you. Peace I leave with you; my peace I give you. I do not give to you as the world gives. Do not let your hearts be troubled and do not be afraid.

" 'You heard me say, "I am going away and I am coming back to you." If you loved me, you would be glad that I am going to the Father, for the Father is greater than I. I have told you now before it happens, so that when it does happen you will believe. I will not speak with you much longer, for the prince of this world is coming. He has no hold on me, but the world must learn that I love the Father and that I do exactly what my Father has commanded me' " (John 14:23-31a).

2. What promise does Jesus make in these verses?

3. What role does the Holy Spirit play in this relationship?

4. What other insights about Jesus did you gain from these verses?

Peter's Words:
"Men of Israel, listen to this: Jesus of Nazareth was a man accredited by God to you by miracles, wonders and signs, which God did among you through him, as you yourselves know. This man was handed over to you by God's set purpose and foreknowledge; and you, with the help of wicked men, put him to death by nailing him to the cross. But God raised him from the dead, freeing him from the agony of death, because it was impossible for death to keep its hold on him . . . God has raised this Jesus to life, and we are all witnesses of the fact. Exalted to the right hand of God, he has received from the Father the promised Holy Spirit and has poured out what you now see and hear" (Acts 2:22-24; 32-33).

1. How does Peter describe Jesus and Jesus' relationship with God?

2. How do the experiences of Jesus affect us?

(10 minutes) After small groups have completed this discussion, ask, "What does the Bible say about a relationship with Christ?" Summarize responses and then say: "God wants all his people to have a relationship with him through Christ. When a person welcomes Christ into his or her life, he or she begins a relationship described in the Bible as 'salvation.' According to the Bible, salvation is both an event and a process.

"What do we mean when we describe salvation as an event?" Listen for explanations that identify an event as "an occurrence or incident, especially a significant one."

Then ask, "What do we mean when we describe salvation as a process?" Listen for explanations that identify a process as "an ongoing movement or progress." Some people may say they've always believed and can't remember a particular time when they committed their lives to Christ.

Tell group members to turn to "My Faith Story: Event, Process or Both?" Encourage them to read the scripture passages, respond to the questions and write their own faith stories in light of what they have read.

My Faith Story: Event, Process or Both?

Instructions: Read the scripture passages under each heading, answer the questions and write your own faith story in light of what you have read.

Event:
"Here I am! I stand at the door and knock. If anyone hears my voice and opens the door, I will come in and eat with him, and he with me" (Revelation 3:20).

"Yet to all who received him, to those who believed in his name, he gave the right to become children of God" (John 1:12).

1. What event begins a relationship with Christ?

2. What part do you play in that event?

Process:
"Not that I have already obtained all this, or have already been made perfect, but I press on to take hold of that for which Christ Jesus took hold of me. Brothers, I do not consider myself yet to have taken hold of it. But one thing I do: Forgetting what is behind and straining toward what is ahead, I press on toward the goal to win the prize for which God has called me heavenward in Christ Jesus" (Philippians 3:12-14).

1. What process does Paul describe here?

2. What is Paul's goal and how does he achieve it?

3. According to Paul, if you aren't perfect, does it mean you're not a Christian? Why or why not?

4. What can you do with your imperfection? What is God's role in this?

The Event and the Process:
In 25 words or less, summarize what you've studied about salvation as both an event and a process.

My Faith Story:
Write a brief faith story, identifying both *events* and the *process* you've experienced in your own relationship with Christ.

After a few minutes ask if anyone would like to share his or her faith story with the rest of the group. If no one volunteers, offer your own to model and motivate others to talk.

(10 minutes) After several people have read their stories, say: "We can see that God is active and alive in our lives. When we make a commitment to Christ and enter into a relationship with him, the Holy Spirit comes to us, teaches us and empowers us to do things we could not or would not do on our own. How is this relationship different from the others we have studied? How is it unique?"

Ask a group member to read 1 John 4:16b-21. Then ask: "How does this scripture passage describe our unique response to God's love? What difference does our relationship with Christ make to the rest of the world?" Listen for responses that acknowledge the need to love and act in response to the love extended to us.

Then say: "Return to your small group and read the 'So What?' worksheet. Brainstorm about resources and needs. Develop both an individual and a group plan of action for using the available resources to meet the needs you discovered. Think about the 'group' as the larger group, not just your three or four people. Discuss individual goals as well. Covenant together to follow up on plans next week and support each other in all efforts."

So What?

Instructions: Read all four steps and try to identify a response to your relationship with Christ. Remind each other of God's presence and support. Draw some conclusions and develop an action plan at the end.

1. List Your Resources

What resources do I have? What resources does the group have? Be specific. One resource you have is the gospel, the good news you can communicate to others. A second resource might be money. How can you use that resource? Think about the group's and various individuals' talents, skills, gifts and time. Build a resource list for both the group and yourself.

Group Resources   **Personal Resources**

2. Evaluate the Needs

In light of these resources and in response to what Christ has done in your life, who could benefit from the resources you listed? Think about individuals and groups of people who could use what you have. For instance, maybe you have neighbors who are currently unemployed and need food. Perhaps your boss is going through marital difficulties and needs to hear some good news about forgiveness.

Identify people who are inextricably tied to you such as your family, friends, co-workers and classmates. What are their specific needs? What resources can be used to meet these needs?

Think about the individuals you don't see or talk to every day such as street people, terminally ill children and famine victims in Africa. What are their specific needs? What resources can be used to meet these needs?

People	Specific Needs	Resources Available

3. Examine Your Own Opportunities for a Response

What will you do personally? Don't try to do it all. Choose one or two situations you've described and decide on a specific, realistic response you can accomplish within one week. Consider the following:

a. What additional information will you need?

b. What strategy will you use to accomplish what you want to do?

c. What will be your first step? the next step? the next?

d. How will you know if you have accomplished what you wanted to do?

4. Set Up an Action Plan for the Group

What can this group do to respond to this unique relationship we have with Christ? We know we can't do it all, but what can we do right now? Choose one or two situations and decide on specific, realistic responses we can accomplish in one week. Consider the following:

a. What additional information do we need?

b. What strategy will we use to accomplish what we want to do?

c. How will we know whether we have accomplished what we wanted to do?

After working in small groups, regroup and discuss plans and ideas. Decide on a plan to reach out to others. Select a task force to decide on and initiate the next few steps. (Note: Whatever is decided probably will take place after the conclusion of this course on relationships. This cooperative effort will be a good way to maintain the group experience and continue to build community. Participants will make a difference as they reach out to the world in response to Christ's love.)

CLOSING

(5 minutes) Ask the group to form a circle. Pass the basket of gloves and mittens and have each person take one. Place the empty basket in the center of the circle. Say: "Each of you has received an unconditional love, the kind of love that will always be there, no matter what you do or say. Think about your relationship with Christ. How do you want to respond to this unique relationship? What can you do to express your appreciation for a love that never changes, a love that never dies, a love that belongs to you just because you have acknowledged its source?

"As you think about this love, think about how you want to respond. When you decide how you want to reach out and show your appreciation for this unconditional love, place your glove or mitten in the basket and say something like, 'I will reach out by checking in daily with the elderly couple who live next door' or 'I will reach out by volunteering my services at the soup kitchen this weekend.' If you choose to reach out in some way that is extremely private to you, just say, 'I will reach out in appreciation for God's love for me.' "

Once everyone has returned his or her glove to the basket, close the session with the following prayer: "God, thank you for the kind of love that reaches out even when we are unlovable. Help us celebrate your love by reaching out to others. Give each of us the ability to translate your love into words and actions that others can understand. We offer these prayers in the name of your Son, amen."

Explain the "Solo" activity for this study and remind participants to bring their Study Guides back to the next session. Encourage everyone to read *More Than a Carpenter* by Josh McDowell (Tyndale). This small book presents historical and theological evidence for believing Jesus was the Son of God and the Messiah.

Let your group members know the final study will concentrate on the unique relationship they have with Christ and how they can develop and maintain their faith.

Instructions: The chart below describes various stages of a person's spiritual journey. Examine the chart and circle the stage that best describes where you are in your own spiritual journey. Then answer the questions that follow the chart.

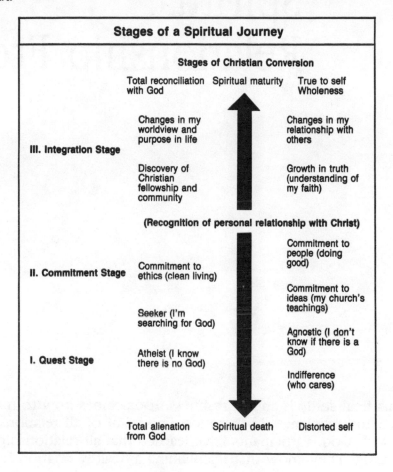

1. Which stages of the spiritual journey have you experienced?

2. What is your most vivid memory about each stage?

3. Which stage are you in now?

4. In which direction do you seem to be moving? Why?

5. What is your next step of faith?

6. How will you accomplish this?

Keeping Your Spiritual Relationship Fresh

*T*his final study is about freshness. It examines how to maintain health and wholeness in that most important of all relationships, the one with God. Participants have learned that all relationships need nurturing. They know that maintaining a healthy relationship demands interaction between two parties. Now is the time to talk about the skills and steps your group members can use for the rest of their lives. This is preparation time, for now and for the future.

As trainer, coach, guide and teacher, you have the opportunity to influence the lives of those people God has put in your group. It's an awesome responsibility, but also an amazing opportunity and a great privilege.

OBJECTIVES

In this study participants will:

● understand that nurturing a spiritual relationship involves specific, intentional steps.

● study the importance of Bible study, prayer, meditation and journaling as they pursue this unique relationship with God.

● evaluate their personal relationship with Christ and decide on concrete steps to make that relationship more vital.

● review what they've learned throughout the studies.

PREPARATION . . . .

☐ Study the material carefully and prayerfully.
☐ Gather newsprint, markers, pencils, Bibles, a large glass bowl and various kinds of fruit.

OPENING

(5 minutes) Welcome the group and say: "Last week we talked about the unique relationship we can have with Christ. Today we want to continue that theme by discussing how we can keep that relationship fresh.

"Look at the fruit in the bowl at the front of the room. What one kind of fruit best describes your spiritual relationship and why? One of you might think your relationship is most like a coconut— hard on the surface, but refreshing once you reach the inside. Another might think your spiritual relationship is most like canned peaches—not as fresh as usual, but still a treat when opened. Which kind of fruit most closely typifies your relationship with Christ?"

EXPLORATION

(5 minutes) After group members have talked about the fruit most like their spiritual relationship, say: "Maintaining a fresh spiritual relationship is much like keeping any other relationship fresh. For example, when you first fall in love, you have no problem keeping a conversation going, writing creative poetry or spending time with that special person. But after you've dated for a while or married that special person, life's daily routines begin to fill your time. Couples discover they have to work hard to find time for each other and maintain the relationship they've had. Keeping a relationship fresh demands 'intentional discipline,' which is two people deliberately setting up guidelines and activities to keep their relationship fresh." Assert examples from your own life or talk about what others have done to maintain a healthy relationship. You might mention that some mar-

ried couples schedule regular date nights or wake up early so they can spend time talking without interruptions.

Continue with: "Even when the immediate freshness wears off, relationships can still progress and be even more vital and alive. The same is true of your spiritual relationship. For example, when you worked on the 'Solo' activity last week, you thought about your spiritual relationship. You examined your spiritual journey, where you have been and where you are now. You also thought about where you needed to go next and how you would accomplish this 'step of faith.' Look back at the 'Solo' activity for Study 11 and see what specific actions you listed. How did you plan to accomplish your next step of faith?"

List responses on a sheet of newsprint. Review this list, pointing out practical, specific steps a person can use to maintain or enhance his or her spiritual relationship.

Then say, "With these thoughts in mind, let's take some time to look at other practical steps we can use to build a better relationship with God."

(10 minutes) Divide group members into two study teams. Assign each team to study one of two aspects for a quiet time: Bible study and prayer. Say: "Turn to 'Keeping the Spiritual Relationship Fresh.' Read the instructions for your team and complete your assignments."

Keeping the Spiritual Relationship Fresh ▬▬▬

Scheduling a daily quiet time isn't just an act of obedience or discipline; it's also an act of love. As you examine the separate components of this special time, remember you are planning a meeting with your best friend, your Savior, your Lord.

A daily quiet time involves several key ingredients: Bible study, prayer, meditation and journaling. Read through the directions for your assignment and complete the activities.

Bible Study

Instructions: Read each of the following scripture passages. List the benefit for studying the Word described in each passage.

 "Your word is a lamp to my feet and a light for my path" (Psalm 119:105).
Benefit for Bible study: _____

_____

 "My son, do not forget my teaching, but keep my commands in your heart, for they will prolong your life many years and bring you prosperity" (Proverbs 3:1-2).
Benefit for Bible study: _____

_____

"Therefore everyone who hears these words of mine and puts them into practice is like a wise man who built his house on the rock. The rain came down, the streams rose, and the winds blew and beat against that house; yet it did not fall, because it had its foundation on the rock" (Matthew 7:24-25).
Benefit for Bible study: _____

"To the Jews who had believed him, Jesus said, 'If you hold to my teaching, you are really my disciples. Then you will know the truth, and the truth will set you free' " (John 8:31-32).
Benefit for Bible study: _____

"All Scripture is God-breathed and is useful for teaching, rebuking, correcting and training in righteousness, so that the man of God may be thoroughly equipped for every good work" (2 Timothy 3:16-17).
Benefit for Bible study: _____

"For the word of God is living and active. Sharper than any double-edged sword, it penetrates even to dividing soul and spirit, joints and marrow; it judges the thoughts and attitudes of the heart" (Hebrews 4:12).
Benefit for Bible study: _____

Read these five steps for effective Bible study and respond to the question that follows.

1. Hear. "He who has an ear, let him hear what the Spirit says to the churches. To him who overcomes, I will give some of the hidden manna. I will also give him a white stone with a new name written on it, known only to him who receives it" (Revelation 2:17).

2. Read. "Blessed is the one who reads the words of this prophecy, and blessed are those who hear it and take to heart what is written in it, because the time is near" (Revelation 1:3).

3. Study. "Now the Bereans were of more noble character than the Thessalonians, for they received the message with great eagerness and examined the Scriptures every day to see if what Paul said was true" (Acts 17:11).

4. Memorize. "My son, keep my words and store up my commands within you. Keep my commands and you will live; guard my teachings as the apple of your eye. Bind them on your fingers; write them on the tablet of your heart" (Proverbs 7:1-3).

5. Meditate. "But his delight is in the law of the Lord, and on his law he meditates day and night" (Psalm 1:2).

How would you recommend a person study the Word to gain the greatest good?

Prayer

Instructions: Answer the following questions by reading the scripture passages that accompany them.

1. To whom should you pray?

"And without faith it is impossible to please God, because anyone who comes to him must believe that he exists and that he rewards those who earnestly seek him" (Hebrews 11:6).

"When you pray, say: 'Father, hallowed be your name, your kingdom come' " (Luke 11:2).

You should pray to _____.

2. Why should you pray?

"Devote yourselves to prayer, being watchful and thankful" (Colossians 4:2).

You should pray because _____.

3. How should you pray?

"But when you pray, go into your room, close the door and pray to your Father, who is unseen. Then your Father, who sees what is done in secret, will reward you. And when you pray, do not keep on babbling like pagans, for they think they will be heard because of their many words. Do not be like them, for your Father knows what you need before you ask him" (Matthew 6:6-8).

"Do not be anxious about anything, but in everything, by prayer and petition, with thanksgiving, present your requests to God" (Philippians 4:6).

You should pray by_____.

4. When should you pray?

"Pray continually" (1 Thessalonians 5:17).

"And pray in the Spirit on all occasions with all kinds of prayers and requests. With this in mind, be alert and always keep on praying for all the saints" (Ephesians 6:18).

You should pray _____.

Kinds of Prayer:

What kinds of prayers should you pray? Identify the kind of prayer as you read each scripture passage.

_____ "Praise the Lord, all you nations; extol him, all you peoples. For great is his love toward us, and the faithfulness of the Lord endures forever. Praise the Lord" (Psalm 117).

_____ "Going a little farther, he fell with his face to the ground and prayed, 'My Father, if it is possible, may this cup be taken from me. Yet not as I will, but as you will' " (Matthew 26:39).

_____ "When they arrived, they prayed for them that they might receive the Holy Spirit" (Acts 8:15).

_____ "Then they cried to the Lord in their trouble, and he saved them from their distress" (Psalm 107:13).

_____ " 'As for us, the Lord is our God, and we have not forsaken him. The priests who serve the Lord are sons of Aaron, and the Levites assist them. Every morning and evening they present burnt offerings and fragrant incense to the Lord. They set out the bread on the ceremonially clean table and light the lamps on the gold lampstand every evening. We are observing the requirements of the Lord our God. But you have forsaken him. God is with us; he is our leader. His priests with their trumpets will sound the battle cry against you. Men of Israel, do not fight against the Lord, the God of your fathers, for you will not succeed' " (2 Chronicles 13:10-12).

_____ "When he had gone indoors, the blind men came to him, and he asked them, 'Do you believe that I am able to do this?'

" 'Yes, Lord,' they replied.

"Then he touched their eyes and said, 'According to your faith will it be done to you' " (Matthew 9:28-29).

_____ "Deliver me, O my God, from the hand of the wicked,

from the grasp of evil and cruel men'' (Psalm 71:4).

_____ "Now when Daniel learned that the decree had been published, he went home to his upstairs room where the windows opened toward Jerusalem. Three times a day he got down on his knees and prayed, giving thanks to his God, just as he had done before" (Daniel 6:10).

Elements of Prayer:

What are some elements of prayer? Identify five elements by reading each scripture passage.

_____ "As for me, far be it from me that I should sin against the Lord by failing to pray for you. And I will teach you the way that is good and right" (1 Samuel 12:23).

_____ "Speak to one another with psalms, hymns and spiritual songs. Sing and make music in your heart to the Lord, always giving thanks to God the Father for everything, in the name of our Lord Jesus Christ" (Ephesians 5:19-20).

_____ "Through Jesus, therefore, let us continually offer to God a sacrifice of praise—the fruit of lips that confess his name" (Hebrews 13:15).

_____ "If any of you lacks wisdom, he should ask God, who gives generously to all without finding fault, and it will be given to him" (James 1:5).

_____ "If we confess our sins, he is faithful and just and will forgive us our sins and purify us from all unrighteousness" (1 John 1:9).

What are some of your general conclusions about prayer?

How would you define prayer?

(10 minutes) Ask each study team to use the next five minutes to prepare a brief report for the other team. Give each group two minutes to report and answer questions.

(5 minutes) After both groups have reported, ask everyone to turn to ''Additional Ingredients for Your Quiet Time.'' Ask participants to meet in groups of three. Then say: ''I'll ask for a report from each group when all groups are finished. You will have five minutes to complete this discussion.''

Additional Ingredients for Your Quiet Time ▬▬▬

Instructions: Read about the additional ingredients of meditation and journaling for your quiet time. Talk about your own quiet times and any insights you might have.

Meditation:

"I meditate on all your works and consider what your hands have done" (Psalm 143:5b). Meditation is defined as "continued thought." During your quiet time, take a few minutes to reflect on what you've digested in your Bible study. You might want to:

- memorize a key verse from what you've studied.
- use a study Bible to analyze what words mean.
- go over the passage several times during the day or the following week.
- place yourself in the passage and imagine what it would be like. For example, if you study the Resurrection, imagine how it would have felt to run to the tomb and find it empty. How would you have responded? Which people would you have wanted to tell?
- think about how you want to respond. Does this scripture passage apply to you? What do you want to do or change as a response to what you've read?

Journaling:

"We write this to make our joy complete" (1 John 1:4). Purchase a small notebook and keep a written record of what God has said to you through his Word. After reading your Bible:

- write the insights you have.
- think about the applications you want to make and write those.
- list the people or situations for which you want to pray.
- record prayers and insights.

After journaling for a few months, go back and see how God has faithfully responded to your cares and concerns.

Have small groups each give a brief report about what they have read. Ask people to offer other insights about meditation and journaling. List these insights on a sheet of newsprint and encourage participants to record them in their Study Guides for future reference.

(10 minutes) Then say: "What happens if you miss a quiet time?" Allow participants to respond to this possibility, then ask them to turn to "When You Miss a Quiet Time . . ." and read the three suggestions silently to themselves.

When You Miss a Quiet Time . . . ▬▬▬▬▬▬

Instructions: Read the following suggestions silently to yourself. Add suggestions you've heard from others.

1. Don't get discouraged. Everyone misses. Don't feel guilty. Simply explain to God that you're sorry, you recognize your need for him and you're looking forward to spending more time with him. He'll understand and accept your explanation.

2. Don't try to catch up. If you've missed several days in a row and been trying to read two chapters a day, don't try to catch up by reading six chapters in one day. Continue your plan, realizing that God doesn't keep score.

3. Relax, and start again the next day. God wants to meet with you. He's certainly not going to begin the meeting by disciplining you for missing yesterday.

4. Other suggestions:

After participants have finished reading and writing, share these thoughts regarding a fresh relationship: "Continuing communication is key to any relationship. If you don't spend time or talk with other people, your relationships deteriorate until you feel awkward and uncomfortable. So spend some quiet time with God each day. The Bible says, 'Pray continually.' Think about what that means. It doesn't mean that you walk around with your head down and your eyes closed. It means you keep communication lines open. Talk to God about what's happening during your day. Think of him as a close, personal friend who is beside you at all times. Recognize and celebrate the presence of the Holy Spirit as he dwells in you.

"Acknowledge your spiritual relationship to others. Jesus says: 'Whoever acknowledges me before men, I will also acknowledge him before my Father in heaven. But whoever disowns me before men, I will disown him before my Father in heaven' (Matthew 10:32-33). Don't be ashamed to talk about your spiritual relationship with others. Discuss the value this relationship has had in your life. When you deny or ignore this unique relationship, you weaken what is there. So live in celebration of your relationship with God and let others know how valuable this relationship is to you.

"Finally, show that you love and care for Christ by obeying his directions. Read diligently and obey the directions you find in the Bible. Study and pray about any uncertainties you have and listen to God as you communicate each day. Obedience breeds trust, and trust keeps a relationship fresh.

"What suggestions would you add for keeping your spiritual relationship fresh?" List these suggestions on a sheet of newsprint and encourage participants to write them in their Study Guides for future reference.

CLOSING

(10 minutes) Encourage group members to think about how their spiritual relationship affects the rest of their relationships. Then ask: "How can you recognize a fresh spiritual relationship within your relationships with others? What specific evidence verifies this unique relationship and its effect on a person's life?"

After individuals have shared their ideas, read the following: "Finally, brothers, whatever is true, whatever is noble, whatever is right, whatever is pure, whatever is lovely, whatever is admirable—if anything is excellent or praiseworthy—think about such things. Whatever you have learned or received or heard from me, or seen in me—put it into practice. And the God of peace will be with you" (Philippians 4:8-9).

Ask group members to reflect on the past 12 weeks—the thoughts and ideas that were especially meaningful to them. Suggest they look back through their Study Guides at significant meetings and think about the personal growth they've made. Ask everyone to choose one significant discovery and share it with the rest of the group.

Conclude this session with the following prayer: "God, we've examined all our relationships. We've opened ourselves to each other and risked rejection. We've listened to each other and found understanding. We've celebrated our achievements and struggled with what to do about our failures. Unite us in our efforts to support one another. And humble us to realize we cannot continue without you. In the name of the Christ whose relationship with you gave each of us the opportunity to be unique, amen."

Explain the "Solo" activity for this study and encourage everyone to complete it even though this is the last study. Explain that this activity will give direction for dealing with the spiritual relationship beyond the study.

Encourage everyone to read *Growing Strong in the Seasons of Life* by Chuck Swindoll (Multnomah). This book is an excellent resource for keeping the spiritual relationship healthy.

Instructions: Where are you on your spiritual journey? Read through the five stages of a spiritual journey. Then examine the areas of your spiritual life. Check a stage for each area to indicate where you are. For example, on "Desire" you might check "Starting" because you have just made a decision to try this relationship with Christ. Think about where you are right now.

Five Stages of a Spiritual Journey

Packing: Getting ready to go, planning, making preparations, thinking it through, making decisions.

Starting: Exploring the terrain, stretching your muscles, experiencing the adrenaline of beginning a new adventure.

 **Climbing:** Pushing your limits, taking risks, straining for high ground, feeling fatigue, suffering pain or discomfort.

Resting: Catching your breath, taking time out, looking back to see where you've been, getting ready for the next push.

Celebrating: Feeling enthusiastic about moving on, recognizing your successes, reaching a specific point.

Where are you?

	Packing	Starting	Climbing	Resting	Celebrating
Areas of your spiritual life:					
Desire: To try a relationship with Christ!	☐	☐	☐	☐	☐
Basic preparation: Getting in shape spiritually.	☐	☐	☐	☐	☐
Stamina: Sticking with the relationship even in rough times.	☐	☐	☐	☐	☐
Stretching: Pushing beyond your limits and liking it.	☐	☐	☐	☐	☐
Belonging: Becoming part of a committed team.	☐	☐	☐	☐	☐
Sharing: Passing along the good news to your friends.	☐	☐	☐	☐	☐

Note: No matter where you are in your spiritual journey, you're in a good place to start. Look over each area of your spiritual life and see where you need to move forward. List ideas on what your next step will be in each area and start walking.

My next steps will be:

Get support for your ministry with these practical resources from

Clear-Headed Choices in a Sexually Confused World

by Terry Hershey

Churches can help today's young adults make responsible personal decisions from a solid Christian perspective. Young adults will better their own sexuality and the choices they have to make by examining . . .

- belief systems . . . ethics and illusions
- what the Bible says about sexuality
- how their personal filters affect the decisions they make
- how to integrate their relationships—with God, others and self

Clear-Headed Choices in a Sexually Confused World offers individuals and young adult groups high-quality study material. The book includes real-life case studies and thought-provoking discussion questions. Young adults will improve their decision-making skills and . . .

- ► avoid black-and-white answers to complex questions
- ► examine the life-giving approach to sexuality
- ► respond to God's grace with life-giving choices
- ► understand our culture's preconceptions about sexuality
- ► build self-esteem through biblical grace

Clear-Headed Choices in a Sexually Confused World is a "must" for every young adult.

228 pages. $11.95
ISBN: 0931-529-30-1

Young Adult Ministry

by Terry Hershey

Here's a professional guide to developing or revitalizing your ministry with young adults, ages 18-35.

Get new insight and effective steps to help you create a flourishing young adult ministry. You'll get a wealth of specific ideas to help build or strengthen your young adult programs.

Plus, you'll get answers to perplexing questions, such as . . .

- ► How do I minister to this diverse age group?
- ► How do I keep up with highly mobile young adults?
- ► How do I revive a struggling young adult ministry?
- ► How do I minister to both marrieds and singles?
- ► How do I find and address young adult needs?
- ► What type of programming works best, and why?

Create your own successful ministry to young adults. Order this specialized professional guide today.

276 pages. $12.95
ISBN: 0931-529-08-5

Friend to Friend

by J. David Stone and Larry Keefauver

Learn a simple yet powerful method for helping a friend sort through a tough situation. The friend-to-friend process is an easy-to-use counseling approach for anyone to help a friend through a problem.

Use it in your own ministry. And teach young adults how to minister effectively to others, friend to friend.

80 pages. $5.95
ISBN: 0936-664-11-8

Training Volunteers in Youth Ministry

Video kit

Give volunteer youth workers a deeper understanding of youth ministry. You'll get expert, in-depth education with the **Training Volunteers in Youth Ministry** video kit. The nation's top authorities on teenagers and youth ministry provide solid, practical information.

Design a complete training program to meet your needs using helpful tips from the 128-page leaders guide and four 30-minute VHS videos . . .

Video 1: Youth Ministry Basics   Video 3: Building Relationships
Video 2: Understanding Teenagers   Video 4: Keys for Successful Meetings

You'll use this valuable resource again and again, sharpening the skills of your volunteer team. You'll discover how to find, motivate and keep volunteers. Plus, you'll strengthen your youth ministry team spirit with practical, affordable youth ministry training.

Video kit. $98
ISBN: 0931-529-59-X

Parenting Teenagers

Video kit

Offer parents needed support for coping with their teenager—through practical video training.

Parents will love the insights and encouragement they get from **Parenting Teenagers**. Offer parents in your church practical communication tips, the whys of rebellion, insights on mood swings, ideas for handling peer pressure . . . plus parenting styles, kids' friends and more. Use **Parenting Teenagers** for years to come in parents' meetings, retreats, Sunday school or even by sending videos home with parents!

Your complete kit includes four 30-minute VHS videos and 144-page information-packed leaders guide full of helpful, ready-to-copy worksheets. Discover . . .

Video 1: What Makes Your Teenager Tick?
Video 2: Parenting: How Do You Rate?
Video 3: Communicating With Your Teenager
Video 4: Your Teenager's Friends and Peer Pressure

Give parents of teenagers the support they need to survive the tough teenage years.

Video kit. $98
ISBN: 0931-529-60-3

Outrageous Clip Art for Youth Ministry

Illustrations by Rand Kruback

Discover off-the-wall cartoons to spice up your newsletters, handouts, brochures, posters and fliers . . .

Tickle the funny bone of teenagers with hundreds of ZANY clip art cartoons. Delight your young people with eye-catching newsletters. Announcements. Handouts. Grab attention fast with out-of-the-ordinary clip art.

Clip art is fast and easy—a cinch to choose, clip, paste and copy. A quick index helps you find a cartoon and the right headline—with many sizes to choose from.

Promote your events with not-so-typical invitations. Use preposterous pictures to boost interest in special occasions, service projects, meetings and much more. Plus, get 335 attention-grabbing ways to announce your events . . .

Burger bash	Pie party	Bus brigade
Roller derby	Water war	Frisbee fling
Lunch munch	Taco fiesta	Pancake feed

and a Bring Your Own Banana—Banana Split Night.

Add spark and spice to all your printed pieces. Boost attendance and excitement—with kid-pleasing cartoons straight from the bizarre imagination of artist Rand Kruback . . .

256 pages. $14.95
ISBN: 0931-529-39-5

The Youth Ministry Resource Book

edited by Eugene C. Roehlkepartain
foreword by Dr. Martin E. Marty

You'll use this comprehensive desk-top reference guide to build more effective youth ministry programs. Prepare youth talks and sermons. And work knowledgeably with young people and their parents.

The Youth Ministry Resource Book compiles vast amounts of data into easy-to-use listings. A detailed table of contents helps you quickly locate resources, contacts and information on hundreds of high-interest topics . . .

● Young people and the youth culture
  (Understand young people better)

● Youth ministry in America
  (Find out who's doing what)

● The youth ministry profession
  (Get the inside information about your colleagues)

● Youth ministry resource information
  (Discover hundreds of books, magazines, videos and films to support your ministry. Plus publishers and distributors—all at your fingertips!)

This complete, easy-to-use treasury of youth ministry data is your best way to stay current with young people and their world.

ISBN: 0931-529-22-0
